SCHOLASTIC

The Great BIG Idea Book
LANGUAGE ARTS

Dozens and Dozens of
Just-Right Activities for
Teaching the Topics and Skills
Kids Really Need to Master

New York • Toronto • London • Auckland • Sydney
Mexico City • New Delhi • Hong Kong • Buenos Aires

Teaching
Resources

Special thanks to the teachers and other creative collaborators
who contributed ideas to this book (in alphabetical order):

Shaun Andolina, Peg Arcadi, Deborah Bauer, Karen K. Bjork, Cheryll Black, Marianne Chang, Sara Everett, Cynthia Faughnan, Ann Flagg, Maryanne Frawley, Rita Galloway, Gail Hennessey, Becky Hetz, Paula W. Hotard, Wendy Kerner, Karen Krech, Jacqueline Kremer, Kathryn Lay, Lorraine Leo, Mack Lewis, Sue Lorey, Lyn MacBruce, Judy Meagher, Ruth Melendez, Evan Milman, Randi Lynn Mvros, Emily A. Olesch, Susan Perkins, Jeannie Quinn, Janice Reutter, Charlotte Sassman, Kathryn Thomas, Sherry Timberman, Andrea Tunnard, Deborah Versfeld, Wendy Weiner, Judy Wetzel, Wendy Wise-Borg, and Janet Worthington-Samo

Formerly published as part of the Best-Ever Activities for Grades 2–3 series:
Vocabulary © 2002 by Jacqueline Clarke; *Writing* © 2002 by Bob Krech; *Grammar* © 2002 by Joan Novelli; *Spelling* © 2002 by Joan Novelli; *Listening & Speaking* © 2002 by Bob Krech

Page 38: "Where Do These Words Come From?" from *If I Had a Paku* by Charlotte Pomerantz. Reprinted by arrangement with the author and Writers House LLC, acting as agent for the author.
Page 41: "Weather" from *Always Wondering* by Aileen Fisher. Copyright © 1991 by Aileen Fisher. Used by permission of Marian Reiner on behalf of the Boulder Public Library Foundation, Inc.
Page 137: "Commas" from *Bing Bang Boing* by Douglas Florian. Copyright © 2004 by Douglas Florian. Reprinted by permission of Harcourt Brace.
Page 174: Poems from *The Pig in the Spigot* by Richard Wilbur. Copyright © 2000 by Richard Wilbur. Reprinted by permission of Harcourt Inc.
Page 222: "Sounds" by M. Lucille Ford from *Poetry Place Anthology* (Scholastic, 1990). Every effort has been made by the publisher to locate the author of this poem and to secure the necessary permissions. If there are any questions regarding the use of this poem, the publisher will take appropriate corrective measures to acknowledge ownership in future editions.

Throughout this book you'll find Web site suggestions to support various activities. Please keep in mind that Internet locations and content can change over time. Always check Web sites in advance to make certain the intended information is still available and appropriate for your students.

Editor: Mela Ottaiano
Cover design by Maria Lilja
Interior design by Holly Grundon
Interior illustrations by Paige Billin-Frye
ISBN-13: 978-0-545-14700-2
ISBN-10: 0-545-14700-X

CONTENTS

CONTENTS

CONTENTS

Introduction

Welcome to *The Great Big Idea Book: Language Arts*! Inside you'll find dozens and dozens of activities, many of which were contributed by teachers from across the country.

The engaging activities in this book provide opportunities to teach and assess language arts skills in fun, creative, and meaningful ways. Many integrate more than one skill from across the disciplines. All of them will enrich your language arts program and support the standards.

The activities are broadly arranged from introductory explorations to more complex applications, drawn from all areas of the curriculum, and provide opportunities for students to work individually, in small groups, and as a class.

Highlights of the book include:

- ideas and activities from teachers across the country

- activities that support the MCREL standards*

- ready-to-use reproducible activity pages, including poetry, games, and graphic organizers

- literature links and related activities

- collaborative writing projects

- test-taking and assessment tips

- suggestions for interactive morning messages

- take-home activities to involve families in student learning

- computer connections

- strategies for English language learners

- multiple-intelligence links, with suggestions for integrating writing, art, movement, and music

- interactive displays

- and many more activities to spark your students' love of language!

The Mid-Continent Regional Educational Laboratory (MCREL) is an organization that collects and synthesizes noteworthy national and state K–12 curriculum standards.

Vocabulary

If you've read *Miss Alaineus: A Vocabulary Disaster*, by Debra Frasier (Harcourt, 2000), you can see the potential for fun in learning vocabulary. That story is about a girl named Sage who mistakenly defines the word *miscellaneous* as "Miss Alaineus: the woman on green spaghetti boxes whose hair is the color of uncooked pasta and turns into spaghetti at the ends." While the story is light and playful, on a more serious note it illustrates the benefits of immersing children in language and wordplay, not only to avoid vocabulary mix-ups but also to prepare students for encounters with unfamiliar text and strengthen their ability to communicate with others. (See page 22 for a related activity.)

This section is designed to liven up your vocabulary lessons while supporting your classroom goals. According to the MCREL standards, students need to understand level-appropriate reading vocabulary, use a variety of context clues to decode unknown words, and use word reference materials to determine the word meaning, pronunciation, and derivations of unknown words. As you use the activities in this section to accomplish these learning goals, you'll find that they naturally accommodate varying levels of language ability.

For example, you can teach students strategies for learning new words in context while reading independently with "I'm Stuck!" Strategies (page 9), Context Clues in Action (page 19), and Comic Clues (page 21). For building skills with language resources such as the thesaurus and dictionary, you'll find Synonym Sing-Along (page 12), Find the Favorites (page 20), and Hink Pinks (page 29). To involve students in setting personal goals, which can include selecting their own vocabulary words, try My Favorite Words (page 11), Student-Selected Vocabulary (page 12) and Word Study Notebooks (page 14).

Word Wall

Create a wall of words to help students build a powerful vocabulary "brick by brick."

Cut out several bricks from red construction paper. As you introduce new vocabulary, write each word on a brick. Arrange the words on a wall in brick formation. Use the wall for word hunts in which students locate words based on a set of clues. For example, find the word that:

- means _____.
- fits in this sentence: _____.
- means the same as _____ . (synonyms)
- means the opposite of _____ . (antonyms)
- sounds the same as the word spelled _____. (homonyms)
- is made up of two smaller words. (compounds)
- is a noun.
- is a verb.
- is an adjective.
- is a pronoun.
- contains a prefix.
- contains a suffix.

Wear a Word

Students try to guess a secret word by listening to team members' definitions.

Write vocabulary words on sticky notes or name tag labels. Place one on each child's forehead (without letting the child see it). Divide the class into teams of five or six students each. On your signal, have team members help one another guess their words by giving definitions. As students guess their words, have them remove the tags from their foreheads. The winner is the first team to guess all of their words.

Sara Everett
Community Christian School
Fort Dodge, Iowa

"I'm Stuck!" Strategies

Prepare students to tackle unknown words with these handy bookmarks. One side features tips for deciphering unfamiliar words. The other side lets students build lists of vocabulary to learn.

- Display a sample paragraph of text that contains one or more difficult vocabulary words. Use the think-aloud approach (see Tip, right) to model the steps listed on the bookmark. (See page 35.)

- Give each student a copy of the bookmark. Have students cut out the bookmark along the dashed lines, spread glue on the back, and fold along the solid line.

- Encourage students to use the strategies on their bookmarks as they attempt to uncover the meaning of new words in books they read.

- Review the other side of the bookmark, "Book Bumps." Explain that reading can become "bumpy" when students encounter difficult words. Have students keep track of their book bumps on this side of the bookmark. Remind them to use the strategies on the reverse side to figure out the meaning of the words they've identified.

Wendy Wise-Borg
Maurice Hawk School
Princeton Junction, New Jersey

Model the thought process you use to figure out the meaning of a word. For example, "Here's a word I don't know. How can I figure it out? First, I'll skip the word and read on while I look for clues." As you review the words on a child's "Book Bumps" list, note that a large number of words may indicate that the book was too difficult. In this case, work together with the student to select the next book for independent reading.

Worn-Out Words

Improve students' writing vocabulary by creating charts of alternatives for overused words.

- Explain that words become "worn out" when they are overused. Give examples, such as *said, big, little,* or *good.*

- Cut out a large pair of jeans from blue construction paper. Write one of the worn out words at the top of the jeans.

- Work with students to cut out "patches" from colored construction paper. Have students record synonyms for the worn out words on the patches and glue them to the jeans.

- Display the chart in the classroom. Encourage students to use it as a resource to liven up their writing!

Judy Meagher
Bozeman Schools
Bozeman, Montana

Cheryll Black
Newton Elementary School
Newton, Pennsylvania

Create new charts for other worn-out words as they come up in students' writing. Try to notice when students use alternatives for these words in their writing.

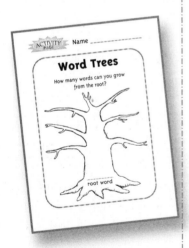

Word Trees

In this activity, students work together to grow words from Latin roots.

- Choose a root word (see left) and write it at the bottom of the tree pattern on page 36. Give a copy to each student. Introduce the root word and discuss its meaning.

- Divide the class into small groups. Have students in each group work together to find as many words as possible containing this root. Demonstrate how to write each word on a separate branch of the tree.

- Provide time for each group to share their word trees. Let the team with the most words choose the next root and repeat the activity.

- As a variation, create an interactive bulletin board. Cut out from craft paper a tree with branches and roots. Staple it to a bulletin board. Write root words on index cards and place one at the root of the tree. Pass out blank index cards for students to record words made from the root. Staple these to the branches.

Root Words

form: shape
script: to write
aud: to hear
port: to carry
dict: to say
cred: to believe

My Favorite Words

Invite students to collect words that are interesting or just plain fun to say!

Explain that writers often keep notebooks to record ideas, quotes, names, or favorite words or phrases. Give each student a small, inexpensive notebook. (Or make notebooks by folding and stapling copy paper.) Model how to collect words. As you read aloud, write down in your own notebook any words that you find unusual or interesting. Tell students why you chose each word—for example, "I like the way this word sounds" or "This word is a wonderful substitute for the word *great*." Let students take turns sharing words they collect in their notebooks. Ask them to tell what they like about each word and give its meaning. Encourage students to use their notebooks as resources for writing.

Literature
LINK

Donovan's Word Jar

by Monalisa DeGross (HarperCollins, 1994)

While some children collect stamps, feathers, or shells, Donovan collects words! When his words (written on small slips of paper) outgrow the jar he keeps them in, he serendipitously gives them away and in the process lifts many spirits. Create a class "word collection jar" that doubles as a positive behavior booster. Work together to record synonyms for overused words, such as *good* or *great,* on slips of paper. Place them in the jar. When students exhibit a positive behavior, reward them with a word!

Synonym Sing-Along

Students use a thesaurus to create new words for old songs.

Divide the class into small groups. Give each group the words to a familiar song such as "Twinkle, Twinkle, Little Star." The song may be the same or different for each group. Challenge groups to use a thesaurus to rewrite the song with synonyms for as many words as possible. Invite them to sing their new versions for classmates. Compile the rewrites into a songbook to be enjoyed throughout the year.

Student-Selected Vocabulary

Use this strategy to create a list of vocabulary words that will help prepare students for encounters with new text.

Give each student a small pad of sticky notes. Ask students to browse the new material. When they come to an unknown word, have them write it on a sticky note and flag the page. On a chart, list the words students identify. To narrow the list, take note of which words were unfamiliar to several students. Choose from the activities listed in this book, such as Wear a Word (page 8) or Gotcha! (page 20), to help students learn the new vocabulary.

Vocabulary Scavenger Hunt

How many vocabulary words can your students find in the media? Send them on a scavenger hunt to find out!

Prepare a list of vocabulary words. Give each student a copy. Challenge students to search through books, magazines, newspapers, and other printed materials to find examples of the words used in context. (You might allow a week for this.) Provide time for students to share their examples with classmates. The winner of the hunt is the student who finds examples of the greatest number of words.

Mix-and-Match Dictionary

Create these dictionaries to help students learn and review a set of vocabulary words.

Prepare a list of vocabulary words. Give students one copy of the dictionary page activity sheet for each word on the list. (See page 37.) Work with students to complete the dictionary page for each word. Have students follow these steps to assemble the mix-and-match dictionary:

- Place the pages in alphabetical order and staple at the top.

- Cut across the dotted line to separate the words from the definitions and pictures.

- Mix up the definition-picture pages so they are no longer in alphabetical order. Staple at the left.

- Use the dictionaries for vocabulary review, having students match the word to its correct definition and picture.

Silly Stories

In this activity, students use vocabulary in context to create fill-in-the-blank stories for classmates to complete.

- Give each student a list of vocabulary words. Have students follow these steps to create their story:

    Write a silly story using all of the vocabulary words.

    Copy the story on another sheet of paper. Replace the vocabulary words with blank lines.

    Look up each vocabulary word in the dictionary. Write its part of speech under the blank line.

- Let students exchange stories and fill in the blanks with vocabulary words from the list. Encourage them to take turns sharing and comparing their silly stories.

Word Study Notebooks

Help students become word wise with these handy notebooks.

Ask each student to bring in a five-subject notebook. Encourage students to use their notebooks as resources for writing, recording words section by section in the following ways:

- Sort new vocabulary into three categories: Words I Know Well, Words I Have Seen Before, and Words I Don't Know.

- Write definitions and/or draw pictures for new vocabulary.

- Create lists of various types of words, such as homonyms, eponyms, and palindromes.

- Collect favorite words. (See My Favorite Words, page 11.)

- Record unfamiliar words (See "I'm Stuck!" Strategies, page 9.)

Create a Word Problem

Students use new vocabulary to create word problems for others to solve.

Give each student a list of vocabulary words. Challenge students to write a math word problem that incorporates as many words from the list as possible. For example: "An enormous ant ate $\frac{1}{4}$ of a scrumptious cake. A famished beetle ate $\frac{2}{4}$ of the same cake. How much did they consume all together?" Let students exchange papers and solve each other's problems.

Rebus Riddles

Work together as a class to create a lift-the-flap book of riddles with compound words.

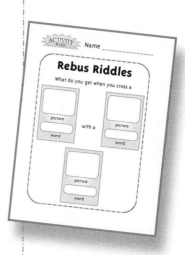

Explain that many new words are formed by putting two words together. These are called compound words. Write several examples on the board. (See Tip, right.) Then give each child a copy of the Rebus Riddles form on page 36, and demonstrate the following steps for completing the sample riddle to learn more about compound words.

⊚ Choose a compound word. In the first two boxes, draw pictures for the two words that make up the compound.

⊚ Write the words underneath each picture.

⊚ In the third box, illustrate the compound as a whole. Write the word underneath the picture.

⊚ Cut out a small piece of construction paper and paste down the top edge over the third box to create a flap.

⊚ Let classmates exchange and read each other's rebus riddles. Then students can lift the flap to check the riddle's answers. Compile them into a class book, or display them in the hallway for others to enjoy.

Sherry Timberman
Homeschool Teacher
Sanford, Maine

Sample Compound Words

milkshake
headlight
sailboat
raincoat
football
horseback
handshake
pancake
earring

Literature LINK

Once There Was a Bull: Frog

by Rick Walton (Gibbs Smith, 1995)

As you study compounds, share this book with students. Each page represents one-half of a compound word and encourages readers to guess the rest. But be warned, a flip of the page often reveals the unexpected!

What's the Password?

Students learn new vocabulary quickly when the words are used as passwords for entering or leaving the classroom.

Use different-colored markers to write four or five vocabulary words on large index cards (one word per card). Post the words by the classroom door. When a student enters or leaves the room, he or she must touch one of the words, say it, and give its meaning. Change the words regularly to help students practice new words.

Rita Galloway
Bonham Elementary School
Harlingen, Texas

Homophone Hold-Up

Play this game to help students distinguish between homophones such as *their, there,* and *they're* or *two, too,* and *to.*

Select a pair or trio of homophones. Have students write each word on a separate index card. Read aloud a sentence containing one of the words. On the count of three, have students hold up the card that they think shows the correct homophone used in the sentence. Write the answer on the board and discuss reasons for that choice. For fun, have students keep track of how many they get right by recording tally marks on a sheet of paper.

Jacqueline Kremer
Chaplin Elementary School
Bozah, Connecticut

Literature LINK

Eight Ate: A Feast of Homonym Riddles
by Marvin Terban (Houghton Mifflin, 1982)

Looking for more examples of homonyms? You'll find a smorgasbord in this book. Share it with students, and then let them create their own riddles from assigned or selected homonym pairs.

Homonyms Are No Joke!

Take advantage of the puns used in many jokes and riddles to teach students about homonyms.

- Share the following riddles:

  > Why did the man name his pig "ink"?
  > Because it kept running out of the PEN.

  > Why is a river wealthy?
  > Because it has a BANK on each side.

- Use these examples to define homonyms (two or more words that have the same sound and the same spelling but differ in meaning).

- Ask students to find a joke or riddle that uses a homonym and to write it on a sheet of drawing paper. Below the joke, have them record the homonyms they used and their meanings. Invite students to illustrate their riddles. Then compile the pages into a class book called "Homonyms Are No Joke!"

Definition Detectives

Can your students positively identify the correct definition of a word when placed in a lineup?

Select six vocabulary words. Have students cut a sheet of paper into six equal pieces. Instruct them to write one vocabulary word on each section. Have them write a definition, either real or make-believe, under each word. Collect the papers for each word and place them in separate bags. Choose five or six definitions for one word from the bag. Write the definitions on the board. Can students identify the real definitions? Repeat for each of the words.

Borrowed Words

English is full of words borrowed from other languages. Use this activity to help students learn the origin of everyday words.

Give each child a copy of the rhyming chant "Where Do These Words Come From?" (page 38) and read it aloud. Let students guess where the words come from. Then explain that they're all derived from Native American languages. Draw students' attention to the bottom of the page. Challenge them to use their dictionaries to discover the language from which each word originated. Encourage students to find other examples of borrowed words. Record them on a chart and display in the classroom.

Answers

Word	Origin
restaurant	French
tea	Chinese
kindergarten	German
pizza	Italian
chocolate	Spanish

ENGLISH Language LEARNERS

This activity provides an opportunity for English language learners to make connections between their first language and English. Extend the activity by helping students identify English words that originated from their native languages. Use the dictionary as a resource. Have them create a poster or mini-dictionary highlighting each word. Encourage them to include both spellings, a definition, and an illustration. Provide time for students to share their work with classmates.

Context Clues in Action

Use this method to teach students how to use context clues to decipher unfamiliar vocabulary.

Give each student a page of text with the last word in each line omitted. Challenge students to identify the missing words using context clues. Ask students to share their answers and explain the strategies used to fill in the blanks. Display these strategies so that students can use them during their daily reading assignments.

Sue Lorey
Grove Avenue School
Barrington, Illinois

Vocabulary Bingo

In this version of Bingo, students review vocabulary words by matching them to definitions.

Give each student a copy of a blank bingo board and a vocabulary list. Have students fill in each square with a vocabulary word. Record the definitions for each word on slips of paper. Place them in a box. Choose a slip from the box and read the definition aloud. If students have the word on their board that matches the definition, they cover it with a marker. Play until one student gets five in a row, across, down, or diagonally.

Jeannie Quinn
Harris Elementary School
Collingsdale, Pennsylvania

Guppies in Tuxedos

by Marvin Terban (Houghton Mifflin, 1988)

What's in a name? This book provides examples of words that originated from people's names. It organizes the eponyms into categories such as food, clothes, and transportation. As a follow-up, let students create an eponym for their names.

Gotcha!

In this game, students use flyswatters to swat pesky vocabulary words.

Make a transparency of a blank bingo board. Write a vocabulary word in each square. Place it on the overhead projector and display it on the board. Divide the class into two teams. Call one student from each team to the board. Give each a flyswatter. Read a sentence aloud, leaving a blank for the vocabulary word. Let players compete to be the first to swat the correct word on the board. One point is awarded for each correct response. The team with the most points at the end of the game wins!

Kathleen Thomas
Woodrow Wilson Middle School
Sioux City, Iowa

Find the Favorites

Sharpen students' dictionary skills with this get-to-know-you activity.

Give each student a copy of the record sheet. (See page 39.) Have students use the dictionary to find and record the guide words that head the page for each of their favorites. Divide the class into pairs and have partners exchange papers. Challenge them to use the guide words to locate the page that lists their partner's favorite in each category. Once they think they've found the actual word, have them write it in the space provided. Ask students to exchange papers once again so they may check and compare each other's responses.

Word Wizards

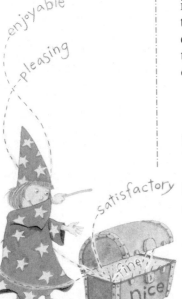

Students become wizards at using new vocabulary in context with this weekly motivator.

- Divide the class into several teams. Let teams choose names such as the Word Wizards or the Vocabulary Vipers.

- Each week, select a new vocabulary word. Write it on the board or another designated spot. Read it aloud with students and discuss its meaning.

- When a student uses the word of the week correctly during a class discussion, award one point to his or her team. You may also want to award points for words used in students' writing, including words from previous weeks.

- After a period of time, tally the points. Congratulate each team on its word power! Encourage teams to set goals for the following week's word. How many more points do they think they can get? How can they work to achieve their goal?

Comic Clues

Use the funny papers to teach students how to decipher unfamiliar vocabulary in context.

Search the newspaper for cartoons that contain unfamiliar vocabulary for your students. Cut out the comic strips, make them into transparencies, and display them on the overhead. Read the comics aloud to students. Ask them to use context clues to predict the meaning of the unfamiliar word(s). Invite those students with correct predictions to share how they figured out the meaning.

Literature LINK

Vocabulary Cartoons: Building an Educated Vocabulary With Visual Mnemonics

by Sam Burchers (New Monic Books, 1998)

This book offers a unique method for learning language. It helps students picture the word using verbal and visual memory cues.

TIP

Subscribe to the Daily Buzzword at **www.word central.com** to receive the word of the day via e-mail. Each entry includes the word's part of speech, definition, usage, and synonyms.

Mini "Me" Dictionary

Improve students' descriptive vocabulary with this dictionary-making activity.

- Give each student a copy of the mini-dictionary reproducible. (See page 40.) Have students cut out each page and write their name on the cover.

- On each page, have students write one adjective that describes them. Ask them to look up each word in a dictionary and record its definition in the space provided.

- Have students place the pages in alphabetical order and staple at the left side. Let students take turns sharing their dictionaries with classmates.

> **ACTIVITY PAGE**
>
> **Mini "Me" Dictionary**
>
> I'm in the dictionary;
> Look and see.
> These are the words
> That tell about me!
>
> by _____
>
> Adjective _____
> Definition _____
>
> Adjective _____
> Definition _____
>
> Adjective _____
> Definition _____
>
> Adjective _____
> Definition _____
>
> Adjective _____
> Definition _____

Vocabulary Parade

Watch words come to life as students create costumes for vocabulary words.

Read aloud *Miss Alaineus: A Vocabulary Disaster*, by Debra Frasier (Harcourt, 2000). This book includes several examples of vocabulary parade costumes. Send home a letter (see the sample in *Miss Alaineus*), inviting students to make a costume that creatively interprets a vocabulary word of their choice. Send home the word list with the letter. In addition, on index cards, have students record their name, word, definition, and a sentence that tells about their costume. Hold the vocabulary parade in the school gymnasium or outdoors. Invite parents and other classes to attend. Read each index card aloud as you introduce students. Take a photo of each costume and create your own vocabulary parade scrapbook.

Words Take Shape

Use concrete poetry to shape up students' understanding of content-area vocabulary.

Share several examples of concrete poetry. A good source is *Doodle Dandies: Poems That Take Shape,* by J. Patrick Lewis (Atheneum, 1998). Assign each student a vocabulary word from a current unit of study. Guide students in creating concrete poems that tell about their word. Display the poems on a bulletin board with the heading "Words That Take Shape." Use the poems for vocabulary review before a unit test.

Math Is Spoken Here!

Encourage students to "talk math" by creating a math word wall.

Brainstorm math words such as *plus, minus, quarter, money,* and *graph*. Write each on a sentence strip and place them on a bulletin board labeled "Math Is Spoken Here." Add new terms as you complete each math unit. Use the word wall for quick review and to help students make connections between different areas of math. For example, the word *quarter* refers to money and fractions and a quarter is one-fourth of a dollar.

Marianne Chang
Schilling Elementary School
Newark, California

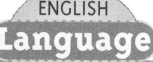

LEARNERS

Create mobiles for number words in various languages, including those of your English language learners. For each mobile, write the number words on separate index cards. Record the words on both sides. Punch holes in the top and bottom of each card. Arrange them in number order and tie with yarn. Hang the mobiles from the ceiling in your classroom. Invite English language learners to use them to teach classmates the number words in their first language.

Vocabulary From A to Z

Use this alphabet game to help students review content-area vocabulary.

Divide the class into small groups. Assign one member of each group to be the record keeper. This student writes the letters A–Z down the left side of a sheet of paper. Give groups ten minutes to record as many terms as they can from their current unit of study for each letter of the alphabet. For example, while studying transportation, "A" words might include *airplane, astronaut,* and *air balloon.* When time is up, let each group read aloud their words for each letter. Have them score two points for each original response (not recorded by any other group) and one point for all other responses. The group with the most points wins!

Gail Hennessey
Harpursville Central Schools
Harpursville, New York

Noisy Vocabulary

Some words make lots of noise!
Use this poem to introduce students to onomatopoeia.

Give each student a copy of the poem "Weather," by Aileen Fisher. (See page 41.) Read it aloud, then introduce onomatopoeia (words that sound like what they mean, such as *ping*). Show students how to use the frame next to "Weather" to create their own sound poems. Provide time for sharing.

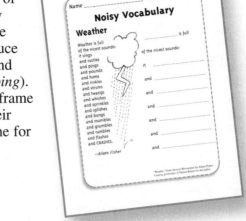

Challenge students to discover more examples of onomatopoeia while listening to a read-aloud or reading independently. Let students record these words on a chart. Display the chart and encourage students to use these words in their writing to appeal to the senses.

Palindrome Puzzles

Show students how words can be symmetrical with this "puzzling" activity.

Write "mom" and "dad" on the board. Explain that these words are palindromes: They are spelled the same backward or forward. Give each student a copy of page 42. Show students how to cut apart, match, and glue the pieces at the bottom of the page to those on top to create six different palindromes. Challenge students to think of palindrome names, such as *Anna, Ava, Bob,* or *Otto,* and record these at the bottom of the page.

Answers

deed	peep
toot	sees
noon	Anna

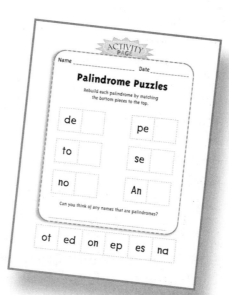

Palindrome Puzzles

Rebuild each palindrome by matching the bottom pieces to the top.

de		pe	
to		se	
no		An	

Can you think of any names that are palindromes?

| ot | ed | on | ep | es | na |

Literature LINK

Too Hot to Hoot

by Marvin Terban (Houghton Mifflin, 1985)

What do you call a firecracker that doesn't explode? A "dud." Find this and other palindrome riddles in this clever book. Share the book and then assign each student a palindrome. Challenge students to create a riddle based on the examples in the book and to share it with classmates. For more fun with palindromes, share *Go Hang a Salami! I'm a Lasagna Hog!* by Jon Agee (Farrar, Straus & Giroux, 1991).

TIP

Invite students to create their own palindrome puzzles! Have them write four- or six-letter palindromes on index cards and cut them apart. Mix them up, place them at a center, and invite students to rebuild the palindromes.

Interactive Morning Message:
Who Has the Word?

Use this cloze technique to integrate new vocabulary into your morning message.

- Choose four or five vocabulary words. Compose your morning message, substituting a blank line for each vocabulary word.

- Cut index cards into strips to fit the spaces left by the blank lines. Record one vocabulary word on each strip. Hand out the strips to students.

- Read the morning message aloud. When you come to a blank line, ask, "Who has the word to complete this sentence?" Show students how to tape the word to the blank line.

- Reread the sentence with the class to see if it makes sense. Ask students to define the word based on context clues and name its part of speech. Use the dictionary to confirm the responses. Repeat the procedure for each word.

ENGLISH Language LEARNERS

Surprise students by incorporating words from different languages (including those of your English language learners) into your morning message. Within the message, substitute English words with words from other languages. For example, instead of "We have music today," you might write, "We have música today." Encourage students to use the context of the sentence to figure out the meaning of the word. Invite English language learners to provide the correct pronunciation for classmates.

Vocabulary Quick-Writes

Here's an easy way to incorporate vocabulary words into journals or quick-writes!

Choose a vocabulary word. Use the word in a writing prompt. Here are some examples:

- difficult — What do you find difficult and why?
- disappointed — Tell about a time that you were disappointed.
- relative — Who's your favorite relative, and why?
- occupation — Describe your dream occupation.

Let students take turns sharing their journal entries. Students' responses should reflect their understanding of the word.

Other People's Words

Use famous quotes to introduce new vocabulary.

Visit The Quotation Page at **www.starlingtech.com/quotes/qotd.html.** Use the search option to type in each vocabulary word from your list. Choose one quote for each word from the search results. Use these quotes to introduce each new vocabulary word. First, read aloud the quote and discuss its meaning. Next, identify the vocabulary word (or have students guess). Let students use context clues to figure out its definition.

TIP

Use these journal entries to assess students' understanding of vocabulary words. Have students who answer incorrectly look up the word in the dictionary and, based on their understanding, write a new response.

An Idiom Feast

Students will enjoy making these mini-books as they learn about idioms.

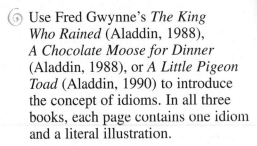

🌀 Use Fred Gwynne's *The King Who Rained* (Aladdin, 1988), *A Chocolate Moose for Dinner* (Aladdin, 1988), or *A Little Pigeon Toad* (Aladdin, 1990) to introduce the concept of idioms. In all three books, each page contains one idiom and a literal illustration.

🌀 Give each student a copy of An Idiom Feast. (See page 43.) Show students how to cut out the pages and staple them together to make a mini-book.

🌀 Read each idiom aloud and discuss its meaning. Let students use crayons or markers to illustrate each idiom literally. Work together with the class to collect and list other idioms that involve food— for example, "bring home the bacon" or "a hard nut to crack."

🌀 Create other idiom mini-books for categories such as colors ("seeing red") or numbers ("two heads are better than one").

Literature LINK

Amelia Bedelia

by Peggy Parish (Harper & Row, 1963)

While teaching about idioms, introduce students to Amelia Bedelia, a hilarious housekeeper who does everything literally. When asked to "draw the drapes," she does so using pencil and paper. When instructed to "dust the furniture," she sprinkles powder all over the furniture and floor. If your students enjoy this book, they'll also love the other titles in the series, such as *Come Back, Amelia Bedelia* (Harper & Row, 1971) and *Thank You, Amelia Bedelia* (Harper & Row, 1964).

Take-Home Activity:
Building Strong Skills

Parents don't always know how to reinforce what their children are learning in school. This take-home letter offers easy suggestions for encouraging vocabulary development at home.

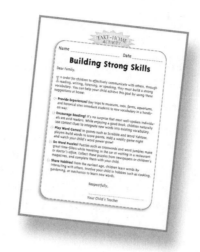

Give each child a copy of the letter on page 44. Read over the ideas for building vocabulary at home. Have children tried any of the ideas before—for example, do some of them play word games at home? Let children share other ways they explore language with their families. As they try some of the activities with their families, encourage them to share their experiences with the class. For example, if they played Scrabble, what was the highest-point word? The longest? The most interesting?

Hink Pinks

What is a riddle with a rhyming answer called? A "hink pink." Students use a thesaurus to solve some hink pink riddles.

Divide the class into small groups. Give each group a copy of the riddles on page 45 and a thesaurus. Set a time limit within which teams are to find the answers to as many riddles as possible. Explain that the answer to each is a hink pink, a pair of one-syllable words that rhyme. Encourage students to use their thesaurus as a resource. When time is up, share the answers (see right) to each riddle, then let children create their own hink pinks.

For more school-home connections, send home the family letter along with a crossword puzzle (if available) or a list of word games that students can check out and take home.

Answers

1. hot pot
2. late plate
3. fat cat
4. swift gift
5. far star
6. dog log
7. bath math
8. wee bee
9. grouch couch
10. roach coach

29

Sample Game Cards

I am feeling nerk.

I walked nerk the stairs.

The football team made a first nerk.

The dress I admired was finally marked nerk.

nerk = down

Nonsense!

Play this guessing game to help students explore multiple-meaning words.

Have students choose a word with at least four meanings, then write on an index card one sentence for each meaning. Have them substitute a nonsense word, such as *moog* or *fip,* for the multiple-meaning word in each sentence. Place the index cards in a bag or box. Choose one randomly and read the sentences aloud. Challenge students to identify the multiple-meaning word.

Pack a Portmanteau

Use this exercise to introduce students to blended words, coined portmanteaus by Lewis Carroll when he said, "You see, it's like a portmanteau—there are two meanings packed up in one word."

Ask students to identify the two words that make up *brunch* (*breakfast* + *lunch*). Explain that these blended words are called portmanteaus, after a traveling bag that opens into two compartments. Give each student a copy of the activity sheet. (See page 46.) Challenge students to use the dictionary to identify the two words that were blended together to create each portmanteau. Share the answers (see below), and encourage students to be on the lookout for other portmanteaus as they read or watch television.

Answers

twirl: twist + whirl
squiggle: squirm + wiggle
smog: smoke + fog
motel: motor + hotel
splatter: splash + spatter
smash: smack + crash

Presto Change-O Letter Tiles

Introduce students to anagrams, and they'll never look at words the same way again!

- Write the word "eat" on the board. Challenge students to rearrange the letters to form a new word (*ate* or *tea*). Explain that words formed by reordering the letters of another word are called anagrams.

- Make copies of the Presto Change-O Letter Tiles record sheet. (See page 47.) Place them at a center, along with a set of Scrabble letter tiles.

- To complete the activity, have students use the letter tiles to form the word in the first column. Then have them read the clue and use the same tiles to create a new word in the third column. Ask them to record the new word in the third column. Then have them remove the tiles and try the next one.

- Challenge students to use the back of the paper to create their own anagrams to share with classmates.

Answers

hint—thin

rate—tear

meat—team

stop—pots

much—chum

loop—pool

Anagrams can also be phrases created by rearranging the letters of more than one word. For example, the letters in "the countryside" can also spell "no city dust here." Find more examples at **www.word smith.org/ anagram/index. html.**

To make your own letter tiles, purchase sheets of 1-inch square ceramic tiles from a home improvement store. Use a marker to label them with letters of the alphabet.

Record each group's performance or video. Replay the video before a vocabulary test to help students review. The videos will also be favorites at open-school night or parent conferences.

Take-Home Activity:
Let's Make Words!

These take-home packs combine spelling and vocabulary as students manipulate the letters of one word to make several new ones.

Make copies of the Let's Make Words! record sheet. (See page 48.) Write a different vocabulary word in the space provided on each one. Place each record sheet in a resealable plastic bag, along with the Scrabble letter tiles needed to make the vocabulary word. Demonstrate the activity by placing the letter tiles for the vocabulary word in order in the space provided. Then rearrange the tiles to make a new word using all or some of the letters. Write that word on one of the lines. Repeat the steps to make as many words as possible. Set up a procedure for signing out the take-home Let's Make Words! packs. Depending upon the materials available, you might want to create duplicate packs for the same word.

Act It Out!

This activity encourages students to find meaning through movement!

Divide the class into pairs or small groups. Assign each group a vocabulary word. Without using the word itself, challenge each group to present its definition to the rest of the class through some form of drama or movement—for example, a skit, pantomime, dance, guided imagery, or body sculpture. Let classmates try to guess the word after each performance.

Wendy Wise-Borg
Maurice Hawk School
Princeton Junction, New Jersey

Kangaroo Words

In his book *The Circus of Words* (Chicago Review Press, 2001), Richard Lederer identifies "kangaroo" words as "big words with little words inside." In this activity students find the "joeys" (little words) inside the "kangaroo" words and connect the two through sentence writing.

⑤ Write a list of vocabulary words on the board. Ask students to identify the "kangaroo" words (those containing little words inside) among them. Record each one on a kangaroo pattern. (See page 49.) Tape the kangaroos to a chart.

⑤ Show students how to find the "joeys" inside each kangaroo word and record them on the pockets.

⑤ Examine each kangaroo word individually. Ask, "Is there a relationship between the meaning of the joey and the kangaroo word?" For example, the word *land* is in *island*. The definition of *island* is "a piece of land surrounded by water." If there is not a direct relationship, let students create one by writing sentences. For example, the word *end* is in *depend*. Students might write, "If Joe can't depend on me, it might end our friendship."

⑤ With each new set of vocabulary words, encourage students to use this mnemonic strategy to help them remember the meanings of words.

Name a Color

We live in a world where color abounds! Yet according to Ariane Dewey, in her book *Naming Colors* (HarperCollins, 1995), only a small number of existing colors have been named. Invite students to expand their vocabulary for colors with this activity.

- Explain to students that paint companies often create names for different shades of color by naming them after something they resemble—for example, sky blue and canary yellow. Share paint strips to provide additional examples.

- Make six copies of the Name a Color activity sheet for each child. (See page 49.) Supply various colors of paper, such as construction paper or gift wrap.

- Let children snip swatches from six sheets of paper and paste one on each page. Under each swatch, have them write a name for the color based on what they think it resembles—for example, snow-man white, Kool-Aid red, or goldfish orange.

- Have students place their pages in alphabetical order and staple them between two construction paper covers (in their favorite color). Let them give their books titles, then add their names as authors. Invite students to share their color books with classmates to discover the different names they gave the same colors.

TIP

Substitute paint for construction paper, and let students mix the colors to create new ones.

Take-Home Activity:
Activity Calendar

Make a home-school connection with these take-home activity calendars!

At the beginning of the month, make copies of the Activity Calendar. (See page 50.) Review with students what they will do at home with the calendars (try one to five vocabulary activities each week). Encourage students to attach any papers they complete as they try the activities to the back of the calendars before handing them in. To create a new calendar for the next month, let each student work with a family member to create a quick vocabulary activity or question for one of the squares. Compile them on a blank calendar grid and make copies for each student.

Name _____   Date _____

I'm Stuck

Use these strategies to figure out the meaning of a word:

- Skip the confusing word. Read to the end of the sentence and look for clues.

- Reread the two or three sentences that come before the confusing part.

- Look for clues in the illustrations or diagrams on that page.

- Think about what you already know about the topic.

- Reread the difficult section one or more times.

- Jot down the word on a sticky note or in your journal if you're still unsure of the meaning.

Adapted from *Reading Strategies That Work,* by Laura Robb (Scholastic, 1992).

Book Bumps

Title:

_____

Word   **Page Number**

_____   _____

_____   _____

_____   _____

_____   _____

_____   _____

_____   _____

_____   _____

_____   _____

Name _____

Word Trees

How many words can you grow from the root?

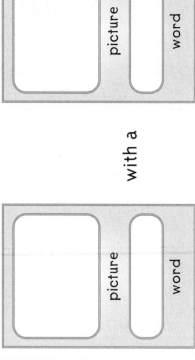

root word

Name _____

Rebus Riddles

What do you get when you cross a

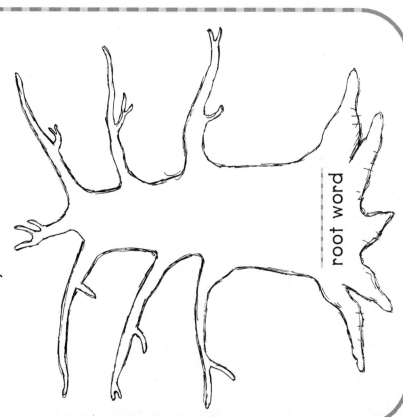

picture

word

with a

picture

word

picture

word

Name _____   Date _____

Mix-and-Match Dictionary

Staple   Staple

Word

✂ cut

Definition

Picture

Staple

_____

_____

_____

_____

_____

Name _____   Date _____

Borrowed Words

Where Do These Words Come From?

Hominy, succotash, raccoon, moose.
Succotash, raccoon, moose, papoose.
Raccoon, moose, papoose, squash, skunk.
Moose, papoose, squash, skunk, chipmunk.
Papoose, squash, skunk, chipmunk, muckamuck.
Skunk, chipmunk, muckamuck, woodchuck.

—*Charlotte Pomerantz*

"Where Do These Words Come From?" from IF I HAD A PAKU by Charlotte Pomerantz.
Reprinted by arrangement with the author and Writers House LLC, acting as agent for the author.

Use your dictionary to list the origin of each word.

Word	Origin
restaurant	_____
tea	_____
kindergarten	_____
pizza	_____
chocolate	_____

Name _____   Date _____

Find the Favorites

Find and record the guide words for each of your favorites. Exchange papers with a classmate, who will use the guide words to locate the page and list the word for each of your favorites.

My Favorite	Guide Words	Word
color		
animal		
food		
sport		
subject		
day of the week		
season		
holiday		
state		
number (1–10)		

Mini "Me" Dictionary

I'm in the dictionary;
Look and see.
These are the words
That tell about me!

by _____

Adjective

_____

Definition

_____

_____

Adjective

_____

Definition

_____

_____

Adjective

_____

Definition

_____

_____

Adjective

_____

Definition

_____

_____

Adjective

_____

Definition

_____

_____

Name _____   Date _____

Noisy Vocabulary

Weather

Weather is full
of the nicest sounds:
it sings
and rustles
and pings
and pounds
and hums
and tinkles
and strums
and twangs
and whishes
and sprinkles
and splishes
and bangs
and mumbles
and grumbles
and rumbles
and flashes
and CRASHES.

—Aileen Fisher

_____ is full

of the nicest sounds:

it _____

and _____

and _____

and _____

and _____

and _____

and _____.

"Weather" from ALWAYS WONDERING by Aileen Fisher.
Used by permission of Marian Reiner on behalf of the
Boulder Public Library Foundation, Inc.

Name _____ Date _____

Palindrome Puzzles

Rebuild each palindrome by matching
the bottom pieces to the top.

| de | | pe | |

| to | | se | |

| no | | An | |

Can you think of any names that are palindromes?

_____

The Great Big Idea Book: Language Arts © 2009, Scholastic Teaching Resources

| ot | ed | on | ep | es | na |

42

An Idiom Feast

by _____

spill the beans
(tell a secret)

icing on the cake
(an unexpected or additional
pleasant benefit)

walk on eggs
(to be careful around
someone or something)

sour grapes
(negative feelings about
something after you discover
that you can't have it)

pie in the sky
(unrealistic)

The Great Big Idea Book: Language Arts © 2009, Scholastic Teaching Resources

Name _____   Date _____

Building Strong Skills

Dear Family,

In order for children to effectively communicate with others, through reading, writing, listening, or speaking, they must build a strong vocabulary. You can help your child achieve this goal by using these suggestions at home:

- **Provide Experiences!** Day trips to museums, zoos, farms, aquariums, and historical sites introduce students to new vocabulary in a hands-on way.

- **Encourage Reading!** It's no surprise that most well-spoken individuals are avid readers. While enjoying a good book, children naturally use context clues to integrate new words into existing vocabulary.

- **Play Word Games!** In games such as Scrabble and Word Yahtzee, players build words to score points. Hold a weekly game night and watch your child's word power grow!

- **Do Word Puzzles!** Puzzles such as crosswords and word jumbles make great time-fillers while traveling in the car or waiting in a restaurant or doctor's office. Collect these puzzles from newspapers or children's magazines, and complete them with your child.

- **Share Hobbies!** From the earliest age, children learn words by interacting with others. Involve your child in hobbies such as cooking, gardening, or mechanics to learn new words.

Respectfully,

_____
Your Child's Teacher

Name _____   Date _____

Hink Pinks

Directions: Use your thesaurus to help you find
the rhyming answer to each riddle.

Riddle	Hink Pink

What would you call a/an...

1. heated pan? _____

2. tardy saucer? _____

3. overweight feline? _____

4. fast present? _____

5. distant twinkler? _____

6. puppy's diary? _____

7. arithmetic done in the tub? _____

8. very small honeymaker? _____

9. grumpy person's sofa? _____

10. insect's car? _____

TRY THIS!
Create your own rhyming riddle:

Riddle _____

Hink Pink _____

The Great Big Idea Book: Language Arts © 2009, Scholastic Teaching Resources

Name _____ Date _____

Pack a Portmanteau

Use the dictionary to find the two words that were
blended together to create each portmanteau.

twirl

squiggle

smog

motel

splatter

smash

The Great Big Idea Book: Language Arts © 2009, Scholastic Teaching Resources

Presto Change-O Letter Tiles

Rearrange the letters in each word to make a new word.
Use the clue for help.

Word	Clue	New Word
h i n t	skinny	
r a t e	cry	
m e a t	squad	
s t o p	pans	
m u c h	friend	
l o o p	swim	

Name _____ Date _____

Name _____   Date _____

Let's Make Words!

How many words can you make from:

1. _____
2. _____
3. _____
4. _____
5. _____
6. _____
7. _____
8. _____
9. _____
10. _____

11. _____
12. _____
13. _____
14. _____
15. _____
16. _____
17. _____
18. _____
19. _____
20. _____

TRY THIS!
Make a sentence using the featured word and at least two other words you made from it. Write it on the back of this paper.

Name _____

Name a Color

Paste color
swatch here.

_____
color name

The Great Big Idea Book: Language Arts
© 2009, Scholastic Teaching Resources

Name _____

Kangaroo Word

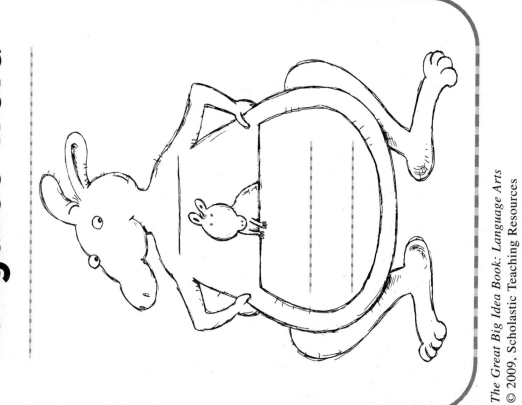

The Great Big Idea Book: Language Arts
© 2009, Scholastic Teaching Resources

Name _____ Date _____

Activity Calendar

Choose _____ activities to do each week. Put a check in the small square when you complete an activity. Return this paper to school on _____.

Make up a nonsense word. What does it mean? □	Name three adjectives that describe you. □	Look up your state name in the dictionary. What information does it tell you? □	Name five words made from the Greek root *ast,* which means "star." □	How many examples of onomatopoeia (sound words) can you find in the funny papers? □
The word *pop* is spelled the same backward or forward. Name other palindromes. □	If your name was in the dictionary, which page would it be on? What are the guide words for that page? □	Use a thesaurus to rewrite a nursery rhyme. □	The graham cracker was invented by a man named Sylvester Graham. Create a food or dish named after you. □	When people say "hold your horses," what do they mean? □
Why was the building never bored? It had a lot of stories! Find other jokes that use multiple-meaning words. □	Name five words that are used as both nouns and verbs, such as *brush* and *plant.* □	Do you have a davenport in your home? Look up the word in the dictionary to find out. □	*Inter* means "between." Create a list of words that use this prefix. □	What is an antonym (opposite) of *crooked?* Name other opposites. □
Complete this analogy: Happy is to smile as sad is to _____. □	*Oatmeal* is a compound word. Check food labels for other compound words. □	How many place names can you find that use the word *new?* Locate them on a map. □	What do these words have in common? *stamp, letter, envelope* □	Name the month. Use the dictionary to discover its origin. □

The Great Big Idea Book: Language Arts © 2009, Scholastic Teaching Resources

Writing

Writing—what an exciting endeavor! It's a method of communicating that allows us to reflect, draw on other sources, and rethink before presenting our ideas—and it has permanence, individuality, and creativity. Kids can be great, motivated writers if they get the support and guidance they need. Though writing is essential and rewarding, it is not always easy. Take, for example, that first step—the blank page. We stare down at it. It stares back. We know we should write. We have plenty to say. But what should it be?

As teachers, we write letters, reports, narratives, and notes, and it is often a challenge to begin that writing. Imagine what it is like for children who have even less experience and mastery of the language. Certainly if we need some support, young writers do, too. The activities in this section are designed to help students grow in confidence and skill as writers. You'll find support for helping students employ a wide range of strategies as they write and use different writing process elements; apply knowledge of language structure conventions, media techniques, figurative language, and genre to create, critique, and discuss print and non-print texts; and adjust their use of written language to communicate effectively with a variety of audiences and for different purposes.

The Writer's Notebook

A writer's notebook is an exciting and productive tool for young writers. Make these notebooks part of students' daily routine to build interest in and frequency of writing.

Obtain an inexpensive spiral notebook or composition book for each student. (Look for sales just before school starts.) They may be ordinary notebooks, but how you present them to students can make a big difference. Before giving students their notebooks, read Byrd Baylor's *I'm in Charge of Celebrations* (Scribner's, 1986). Ask why the notebook in the story is important to the young girl. What did it do for her? How could a notebook be helpful to a writer? Record class responses on the board. Suggestions might include brainstorming story ideas, keeping notes about interesting things, jotting down bits of conversations, writing rough drafts, and keeping a diary. Ask students to write down two or three ways they would use a writer's notebook if they had one. Only then distribute a notebook to each student. Tell students you will collect notebooks once a week and will look forward to reading their ideas.

Schedule notebook review days and collect only a few each day. This way you can enjoy reading them rather than face a huge stack that soon becomes a chore.

We Could Write About That

Writers are always looking for ideas, and sometimes ideas occur to us at the most unlikely times. We learn the hard way that if we don't write them down, they slip away. Help with this by maintaining a Writer's Idea Chart in your classroom.

Label a sheet of chart paper "Writer's Idea Chart." Keep a marker next to the chart (or tie one to a string and tape it to the chart). When a potential writing idea or topic comes up, let students record it on the chart. Keep the chart low enough so that students can add to it as things occur to them. Leave it up as a continually expanding reference for everyone.

Charlotte Sassman
Alice Carlson Applied Learning Center
Fort Worth, Texas

Timely Topics Bulletin Board

Want to create a popular interactive bulletin board? Try a "working" bulletin board that will support your class writing program.

- Cover a bulletin board with roll paper and set up a table in front of the board. Choose a topic or theme students are working on. It could be something as broad as "Autumn" or as specific as "The *Titanic*."

- Announce the focus or theme of the board to the class, then pass out art materials and strips of adding machine paper to groups of students. Ask students to decorate the paper with art and vocabulary that fit the theme.

- When students are finished, have them tack their strips of paper to the board to create a border. As the unit develops, encourage students to add relevant vocabulary, ideas, news articles, poems, and pictures to the bulletin board.

- To enhance learning about the theme, invite students to use the table in front of the bulletin board to display items they bring in or create. When the time comes to write, students can use the display to gather information and inspiration for their writing. It's a great resource that grows as the unit does.

Judy Meagher
Student Teacher Supervisor
Bozeman, Montana

Picture This

How to begin? This is something all writers, from Tom Clancy to new second-graders, face. Try this literature-based art activity to give students a place to start.

- Share examples of successful beginnings by favorite authors. *Verdi*, by Janell Cannon (Harcourt Brace, 1997), is a good choice:

    > *On a small tropical island, the sun rose high above the steamy jungle. A mother python was sending her hatch-lings out into the forest the way all mother pythons do.*

    > *"Grow up big and green—as green as the trees' leaves," she called to her little yellow babies as they happily scattered among the trees.*

- After reading this sensory-rich beginning, ask students to visualize the island and then draw pictures of it. Explain that Janell Cannon, the author, says that her stories almost always first appear to her visually. She sketches a series of drawings that create the structure of the book, then, using those images, writes a first draft.

- Invite students to try the same technique to start a new piece of writing. Have them picture the way they want their story to begin and then sketch it. Their pictures will give them something concrete to go on when it's time to write, easing the way to writing great beginnings.

Adapted from *Teaching Story Writing: Quick and Easy Literature-Based Lessons and Activities That Help Students Write Super Stories* by Joan Novelli (Scholastic, 2000)

Literature LINK

On the Bus With Joanna Cole: A Creative Autobiography

by Joanna Cole with Wendy Saul (Heinemann, 1996)

In this informative picture book, Joanna Cole, the author of the popular Magic School Bus series, tells about her development as a writer and the writing process behind the Magic School Bus books. It's a good book to use to point out to students that yes, even the professionals go through a writing process, make mistakes, and have to edit. Just like the rest of us, published authors experience struggles with writing.

Fishing for Topics

A fish bowl filled with fun writing ideas is the inspiration for quick speeches that students prepare and present.

- Write fun writing topics—for example, "My Life on Mars" or "Why Chocolate Should Be Eaten at Every Meal"—on slips of paper and fill a fish bowl with them.

- Have groups of four or five students pick one paper apiece from the fish bowl. Give students time to create a two- or three-minute speech on the topic. They can write notes on index cards.

- At the end of the writing session, let students share their speeches. Do only a few at a time. This works great as an activity choice when setting up center rotations. After a while, have students submit topics to you for inclusion in the fish bowl. These can become very creative!

Lyn MacBruce
Randolph Elementary School
Randolph, Vermont

Spooky Story Organizer

Kids love spooky stories—listening to them, reading them, and writing them. Don't save this story-starter activity for Halloween. Kids will love it anytime!

Give each student a copy of the Spooky Story Organizer. (See page 80.) This haunted house has windows that open for all the important story elements: character, setting, and plot outline. Guide students in setting up the organizer. Have them cut along the dashed lines to make window flaps that open and then glue the house to a sheet of construction paper around the edges only. Students can add other touches as they like, drawing spooky creatures, webs, and so on, for effect. Have them use the organizer to outline their thoughts as they plan their own spooky story. As students complete their stories, you may want to schedule a candlelight reading . . . if you dare!

Super Story Board

Sometimes young writers have many valuable ideas within a story but experience difficulty keeping the ideas organized and the events in a logical sequence. Use the Super Story Board (see page 81) to help.

- Explain that often it is very helpful to make brief notes and/or sketches about a story to develop a simple structure and sequence of events before actually writing.

- To demonstrate this, read aloud a picture book (any of the Kevin Henkes mouse stories will provide a clear and simple sequence of events). Follow up by using a copy of the Super Story Board to outline the story from beginning to end. Invite students to help with the process. As they recall major scenes, record them on the story board with words and simple pictures.

- Give students blank copies of the story board to complete for stories they're planning. This prewriting activity can help students sequentially think through their ideas and plot out stories ahead of time, making the writing experience much more productive.

Interactive Morning Message:
Daily News Skill Builder

Welcome students to school with a morning message that invites them to write about and share important news.

As part of your morning message each day, invite a few students to record their "news" for the day (on the chart paper below your morning message). Let students read aloud their news during the morning meeting. After each child reads, say something like "Let's look at what [child's name] has chosen to do in [his/her] writing." Reflect on the news content as well as the writing conventions the student used, such as capitalization and spelling. This reinforces skills and gives students an audience for their writing—all in just a few minutes each day!

Jacqueline Clarke
Cicero Elementary School
Cicero, New York

A Character Is Born

Many authors share the view that the characters they create really dictate how a story will develop. Some write pages of biography on characters, so that they know them intimately before seeing what they will do in a story. Here's an activity that lets students try the same technique.

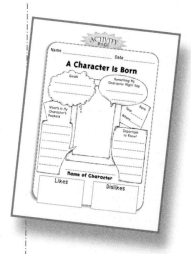

- Begin by discussing a favorite character in a book the class is reading. List information students share, trying to elicit concrete details, such as the character's name, age, and home, as well as more abstract ideas, such as strengths and weaknesses. Ask students to tell how these details relate to the story. (For example, is the age of the character important? Why?)

- Give students a copy of page 82. Have them notice ways in which they can use the page to develop a character by name, physical characteristics, family background, important past experiences, likes, dislikes, friends, environment, and other important information they might want to add.

- Have children complete the activity sheet to explore their character. Once the character is "born," students can include him, her, or it in the writing process as they develop their next piece.

TIP

Go further by inviting students to introduce their characters to the class before writing. Feedback from peers can help them develop the sorts of experiences such a character might become involved in. Children can gather some great story suggestions in this way.

The Phone Call

Good dialogue in a story makes us feel we are right there in the scene, but to write it well requires listening to the conversations around us. Try this activity to focus on this important aspect of writing.

Have students create characters with the A Character Is Born activity. (See above.) Then pair them up to write a phone dialogue between their two characters. They can choose a topic for the conversation, or you can assign one. Have students work on the conversation together, considering how their characters would sound on the phone, including accents, word choices, slang, syllables, beats, pauses, attitudes, mood, objectives, and problems. Ask students to write out the whole conversation and make two copies. Then have students pair up to present their conversations in class, using cell phones as props. Reading the conversation aloud like this is a great test of the authenticity of dialogue.

TIP

Once students have generated a few of these lists, invite them to choose a favorite and use it as the subject of a story. The items on their lists will provide ready-to-use details for their story writing.

List-a-Mania

A favorite writing activity with second- and third-graders is list-writing. Children find list-writing nonthreatening. Often they don't even see it as writing—yet it very much is. Here's a way to turn those lists into more involved pieces of writing.

Invite students to make a list of something—for example, ten things that are noisy, ten things that smell good, ten things that go splat, or ten kinds of carnivores. Lists can be simple, one- or two-word entries at first, but you can lead students to develop their topics—for example, "Ten reasons we should (or should not) wear school uniforms" or "Eight sentences explaining why I think we should have recess twice a day." You can connect list-writing with curriculum areas—for example, "Eight sentences describing the main character" or "Five sentences describing the characteristics of insects." As students become more accomplished at making lists, they can use them to construct topic sentences and supporting details or arrange them to create an outline for a paragraph.

Mack Lewis
Sams Valley Elementary
Central Point, Oregon

ENGLISH Language LEARNERS

Predictable patterns are helpful to English language learners in both reading and writing. For a writing lesson built on predictable patterns, share *I Hate to Go to Bed*, by Judi Barrett (Four Winds Press, 1977), a story that lists the many reasons the narrator hates to go to bed. But if she has to, well, there are some good things that come out of it and she lists these as well. Have students choose one thing they hate to do and list eight reasons they hate to do it. Give students nine blank pages and ask them to write (or dictate) and illustrate, on separate pages, what they hate to do and why (eight reasons). Pass out a tenth page. On this page, have students write (or dictate) "But, if I have to . . . [whatever it is], then . . . " Give students eight more pages and have them write (or dictate) ways in which it can be a good thing, again with one reason per page. This easy and fun format results in a humorous picture book.

Super Story Starters

Leads or beginnings of stories are often answers to questions—for example, they might answer the question "Where does this story take place?" (*The house stood lonely at the top of the hill.*) or "Who is the main character?" (*John Smith was an old man, gray and bent.*) Use this activity to help students create engaging possibilities for a lead that helps answer readers' questions.

- Pair up students and ask them to think about a scary thing that has happened to them. Have each student write three sentences, with a maximum of ten words in each sentence, to convey the story.

- Ask students to take turns reading aloud their stories to each other—but they can read only the three sentences. While one student tells the story to his or her partner, the other student listens, then writes down five questions that will help flesh out the story. The listener gives the questions to the teller, then the two students switch roles.

- Have students answer the questions their partners asked and then use this information to help create leads for their stories when it's time to write.

Adapted from "Growing Leads" in *AFTER THE END: TEACHING AND LEARNING CREATIVE REVISION* by Barry Lane (Heinemann, 1993).

Buddy Interview Outline

Sometimes it can be a challenge for students to get to know each other at the beginning of the year. The Buddy Interview uses writing to help the process.

The interview outline on page 83 includes a variety of prompts as well as space for children to add their own questions. Give each student a copy of the outline, and assign partners. Have partners meet and interview each other, using the outline to take notes. As students complete their interviews, have them review each other's work. When everyone's finished, have each set of partners take turns introducing each other, using their interview outlines as a guide.

Friendly Want Ads

Want ads are in almost every newspaper and they're often very interesting to read. There are want ads for just about everything, including pets, cars, bikes, books, and help. Writing want ads gives students practice with using specific language and being brief. In a twist on want ads, have students write an ad that describes a friend they'd like to meet.

- Begin by letting students take a look at published want ads—for example, the employment section. What words do people use to attract potential employees? What words do the writers use to make the job description clear?

- Ask students to think about words that describe a good friend. Invite them to share the kinds of things they want to find in this friend—for example, a shared interest in sports, movies, activities, or books.

- Remind students to focus on word choice as they create their want ads. Have them type up their final ads using a font and size that give the ad a newspaper look.

Sue Lorey
Grove Avenue School
Barrington, Illinois

Have students trim the ads to size and arrange them in column format (as in a newspaper) on a large sheet of newsprint. Display students' classified ad sections on a bulletin board. Use the ads as discussion starters for how to be a good friend. Notice the variety of words students use to describe good friends.

Poetry for Writing

Ask students whether they have ever had trouble coming up with ideas about what to write. Let them tell about various obstacles they encounter. Then share a poem that focuses on this problem.

Give students copies of the poem "Just Write." (See page 84.) Read it aloud, then discuss what's happening and who's talking. What was the student's problem? What did the teacher in the poem do to help? Brainstorm ways to get creative juices flowing when writing. Chart these ideas and display for future reference and inspiration. Read the poem again, this time dividing the class into two groups—one to take the part of the teacher, the other to take the part of the student. Students may also enjoy partnering up and reading the poem again, with each child taking one of the parts.

Pick a Label

A bagful of wrappers and labels from candy bars, gum, canned foods, cookies, cereal, and other household items is the start of this fun writing exercise.

- Ask students to save and bring in labels. Place them in a bag.

- When you have a good assortment, let students take turns selecting a label at random from the bag. Divide the class into groups and give each group a sheet of chart paper or posterboard. Let students work together to create a piece of writing that weaves together the words on their labels.

- When they want to use the label word, have them glue down the label instead of writing it. Encourage an open-ended approach to the project. Students might develop an advertisement, write a letter, or create a story or poem. This is a fun opportunity to write as a group and get very creative.

Sue Lorey
Grove Avenue School
Barrington, Illinois

TIP

If you plan to repeat this activity, you may want to trim and laminate labels and wrappers, then glue them to cardboard so they will stand up to frequent use.

Literature LINK

Shh! We're Writing the Constitution

by Jean Fritz (Putnam, 1987)

Writing as a group is not always an easy task. Just ask the representatives who drafted the U.S. Constitution! This book provides an interesting look at the process and includes fascinating facts about the Constitution and the people who wrote it. After reading and discussing the book, have students meet in small groups to write a class constitution. After each group has created a draft, bring students together to negotiate, edit, and write a class constitution everyone can agree to and sign.

The Math Problem Monthly

In math as in any subject, it is important for students to understand what they are doing and why they are doing it. Unfortunately, many young mathematicians memorize procedures or methods without understanding the concepts supporting them. Address this with the Math Problem Monthly—a collection of student-written math problems.

- Each month, have students write a word problem that would require the reader to use a target math concept.

- On the back of the paper, have students write about how to solve the problem. Ask students to include the answer as well as illustrations and diagrams, as needed.

- Have students trade papers with a partner to check their work and make sure the writing is clear and the answer complete.

- Put several problems together on a page, then photocopy and bind them. Place students' originals, which include answers, in a binder so that students can try the problems and check their answers.

Take-Home Activity:
Recipe Writers

Writing recipes may sound easy, but it's not quite so simple. As students learn from this activity, they must combine clear writing of directions with lists of measurements and materials, while trying to keep the style interesting and engaging.

Give students a copy of page 85 to take home. Have students ask a family member who cooks to explain how to make a favorite dish. Tell students to take notes on a sheet of paper and then use the Recipe Writer form to write up the recipe. Students can enhance their recipes with illustrations. Compile finished pages into a yummy class cookbook students will enjoy browsing.

What Are They Writing About?

Students create mini-mysteries for their classmates to solve.

Have each student select an object. It can be as simple as a button or as important as the Statue of Liberty. Have students observe the object carefully (either firsthand or through photographs, videos, and books) and write notes detailing physical characteristics, such as color, size, and texture. Ask them to note other important attributes, such as how the object makes them feel. The only thing they can't mention is the name of the object. They should write this on the back of the paper. Place students' completed descriptions in a box. Take time each day to let students randomly choose one and share it with the class. (Be sure to keep the answer on the back of the description out of view.) Who can guess the object from the description?

Classroom Comics

Use students' interest in comic strips to inspire their own humorous writing.

Invite students to share comic strips they've read. What do they like about the pictures? About the writing? Use correction fluid to white out the word balloons on favorite comic strips. Invite students to suggest new dialogue to complete them. Let them follow the format to create original comics, combining illustrations with dialogue in word balloons. Students might like to publish their comic strips newspaper style, arranging them on a large sheet of paper.

Class Feedback Box

This activity gives students a practical outlet for writing about relevant topics and lets you know how they feel about their school experience.

Make a Class Feedback Box by covering a shoe box with decorative paper and cutting a slit in the top. Tape the lid to the box. Label the box and place it in an accessible spot. Introduce the box to students, explaining that you are interested in getting feedback about the class—for example, about homework, tests, lessons, and social conflicts. Ask students what kinds of things they think you might want to know about. Topics such as homework, tests, pace of lessons, and social conflicts will likely emerge. Invite students to write about their comments and concerns and place them in the box.

Feedback entries do not have to be signed but can be, especially if students want you to get back to them about the issue.

How Do You Do It? Guides

Most of the writing kids will grow up to do on a regular basis is also nonfiction. It's always good to have experience writing in this way. One fun way to do this is to invite kids to write their own guidebook to something they know how to do well.

Share some "how-to" guides with students. Ask students to suggest three guidebooks they could write. Encourage them to be creative—as you know, there are guidebooks on almost every conceivable topic! Possibilities include hobbies (collecting, gardening, bird-watching), sports (swimming, baseball, basketball), and recreation (bike riding, fishing, camping). Conference with students and help them select one topic and then write an outline or web of the main points they'd like to share about their area of expertise. Have students use their notes to write and illustrate their guides, which will make great additions to the class library.

And the Next Book in the Series Is . . .

Kids in grades 2 and 3 seem to gravitate toward series. Favorites include The Magic Tree House, Arthur, Polk Street School, and Time Warp Trio. It's fun to get to know the characters from one book in a series to the next and follow them on their new adventures. How exciting for students to come up with their own addition to a series!

As students read books in a series, they become familiar with the style, conventions, and characteristics of the author and the main characters. As a highly motivating writing project, invite students to write the next book in one of their favorite series. Have them begin by listing what is similar and consistent throughout the series they select. Using these ideas as a guide, have them create a new story in the series. These are immensely fun to write and share. Of course, a natural extension is for students to get started on their own series. Do they have a favorite character from a story they've written who can come back in a new adventure? That's the start of a series!

It's the Same, It's Different!

This collaborative writing project invites students to experiment with ways to share their work with an audience.

Work together as a class to create a piece of writing. A poem, descriptive paragraph, or short story are all good options. Ask students to think about how they could share this piece of writing. Writing and printing it on the computer (or in neat handwriting) is an obvious choice. But how about sharing it through a musical presentation? Visual art, drama, computer graphics, and dance are other options. Divide the class into groups based on their preferences for presenting the piece. Schedule a time for each group to work and later to present to the rest of the class. Discuss how each presentation allowed students to use different ways of "being smart" to share their work.

Advertising Campaign

This cooperative and creative project can encompass a variety of writing abilities, letting all students shine as they become more savvy consumers.

- Begin by asking students which stores they like going to and which products they are most interested in. List these on the board. Share advertisements from newspapers and magazines, noting any that feature stores or products students mentioned. Ask students to bring in their own samples of print advertising. What elements do ads have in common? What are some features of favorite ads?

- Divide the class into groups, and have each group decide on a product they would like to sell or a store they would like to "run" together. Have students work together to create an advertising campaign that will promote their product or store.

- As part of the campaign, have students create a one-page magazine advertisement with text and illustrations. The campaign could also include songs, music, poems, jingles, video, or radio recordings.

Shaun Andolina
Village School
Princeton Junction, New Jersey

Take-Home Activity:
What a Time We Had Together!

This activity is designed to foster school-home connections while encouraging family sharing and writing.

Label a large resealable plastic bag "Take-Home Writing Pack." Place a laminated copy of page 86 (the family letter), some lined writing paper, and two special Writing Together pencils (pencils with fun erasers, curly ribbon tips, or other suitably fancy extras) in the bag. Explain that students need to talk with a family member about an activity or event they enjoyed together—for example, making a birthday cake for a sibling, picking out a new pet, or reading a favorite book together at bedtime. They then brainstorm other details of that day or evening, such as the weather and who was there. Finally, parent and child each write a story about the event, then help each other edit their pieces before writing final drafts. Children return their final drafts to school (parents may keep theirs) along with the rest of the packet. Students can share their stories by reading them aloud, by adding them to a class anthology, or by displaying them on a bulletin board.

Literature LINK

Arthur Writes a Story
by Marc Brown (Little, Brown, 1996)

When Arthur's teacher asks students to write a story about something important to them, Arthur immediately knows that he wants to write about how he got his puppy, Pal. Unfortunately, he soon begins to listen to other story ideas his friends have come up with and, rather than stick with his original idea, he tries to incorporate everyone else's suggestions into one huge stew of a story—with pretty funny results. Arthur learns two important writing lessons: Write what you know and care about, and don't try to do everything in one story. This book can be a good springboard for a discussion on difficulties in writing. What kinds of problems do the writers in your class face?

Writing to a Picture Prompt

More and more national and state writing assessments include writing to a prompt. The writing is timed and students are told simply to write about the prompt. Many students are not used to being asked to respond in this way and because of this lack of familiarity may have trouble demonstrating their true writing abilities. Help them prepare for and practice this type of testing with this activity.

- Look through magazines, newspapers, or books for pictures and illustrations that could be used as picture prompts. Cut out and photocopy several pictures.

- Give each child a copy of one of the pictures (keep the other pictures handy for repeat practice), and supply writing paper and a pencil.

- As might happen on a test, tell students that they will have 15 minutes to write about the picture. Make clear that there is no single correct response but that the writing students do should be thoughtful, with good detail, organization, punctuation, spelling, and grammar.

- Practice the activity repeatedly. Let students compare their writing from one picture prompt to another to notice areas of improvement.

Literature LINK

Writing It Down

by Vicki Cobb (J.B. Lippincott, 1989)

We think a lot about the writing we do, but what about the tools we use to do it? Writing tools didn't always exist. This picture book takes a look at the instruments of writing, including paper, ballpoint pens, pencils, and crayons. It investigates the history of how these items were invented as well as how they actually work.

TIP

Remind students that if an assessment is timed, they need to keep an eye on the clock and should always save some time for self-editing.

Parent Newsletter Writers

It's a very valuable practice to communicate with parents through a monthly or weekly newsletter or regularly updated Web site. This same newsletter is a great way for students to publish their writing.

At least a week in advance of sending each newsletter home, assign students a piece of the newsletter to write. It could be a review of a book they've read, or a poem, short story, report, or other written material that will help inform parents about what's happening in the classroom and update them on events. This gives student a real venue for their published work and will provide parents with insight into student work and thinking at that grade level. Everybody benefits.

Interactive Morning Message:
The Five-Minute Answer

Most students come to school eager to share something. This morning message gives every student a chance to start his or her day sharing—and writing.

Before students come into the classroom in the morning, write a question on the morning message for them to respond to. It could be as simple as "What did you do last night between 5:00 and 7:00 P.M.?" or as thought-provoking as "Where do you want to be living when you are twenty-five years old, and why?" Have students write for five minutes about the question. You can take time to share answers in a discussion or have a bulletin board for posting answers. Make sure you write a response, too!

Save your completed newsletters on a disc. Many of the items you discuss in them will remain the same from year to year. Keep them in chronological order and put them to use as templates each year.

You Know Me at Home, but . . .

This activity makes a great open-school night or conference time icebreaker and encourages children to share information about school with their families.

- Give each child a copy of the form on page 87. Have children use words and a picture to create a portrait of themselves. Children will fill in details about themselves and draw a mini self-portrait in the picture frame area.

- To complete the form, have students cut around the "My name is" flap along the dashed lines. Have students glue their papers around the edges only to a sheet of construction paper and write their name under the flap.

- Display the portraits on a bulletin board. At open-school night or conferences, challenge parents to find their child's picture. (They can lift the flaps to check their guesses.) All of the writing prompts and questions deal with school-oriented activities that families might not know much about, which makes the activity interesting and more challenging for parents.

Karen Bjork (retired)
Portage Public Schools
Portage, Michigan

ENGLISH Language LEARNERS

For many English language learners, there are not only language adjustments to be made but also cultural conventions to learn. One such convention has to do with writing letters, notes, and invitations. Provide students who are new to the English language and culture good models of the elements of a letter or invitation. Look not only at elements such as greeting and date but also at the subtleties of these forms of writing—concepts such as writing in a "polite" way and deciding when these sorts of letters and invitations are appropriate or important. In addition to reviewing the elements of these models, you may want to select a class event like a play or field day and have students write invitations to their families and friends. Use or make fancy notepaper, and allow space for illustrations. Children will really enjoy the process and the results when their invitations are accepted by their guests!

Robot Instruction Writing

As teachers, we are always giving instructions. Students love having a turn at this, and it can be a good opportunity for practice in clear thinking, reading, writing, and listening.

Have students work in pairs. One student is the instructor; the other is the robot. The instructor chooses a simple task for the robot to do. It might be tying a shoe or adding two numbers together on paper. The instructor must write out instructions on how to do this task. The instructions must be very clear and specific because the "robot" can only do exactly what the instructor says, no more, no less. The robot listens carefully to the instructions and follows along. The instructor may need to adjust instructions after seeing the results of the first trial. After several trials, have partners switch roles. This is fun for all, and it really helps students see the need for specific, clear instructions.

What's Good? What's Better?

Children learn to look objectively at their writing by critiquing peers' writing—no names attached.

Using quality children's literature is a great way to model elements of writing. But the level at which many students write is far from the likes of E. B. White, Roald Dahl, and other favorite authors. In addition to using literature to model writing skills, share samples of peer writing. Save samples of students' writing from year to year and copy them on chart paper or make transparencies (leave off names). For quick reference, label them with the various skills they exemplify. Share the pieces with students and ask, "What's good about this piece? What could be better?" Model this process frequently. As students answer these questions about writing selections by peers, they'll learn to look at their own pieces in the same way. During their writing conferences, students will be better able to answer these questions.

Jacqueline Clarke
Cicero Elementary School
Cicero, New York

Works in Progress

There are many steps in the writing process and lots of writing going on in your classroom. The Writing Workshop Record form is one way to keep this information organized.

Give students copies of page 88. At the end of each writing session, have students fill out the form to keep you informed about the status of their writing. There is space for you to add additional checkpoints and comments. Students can hand these in to you or keep them in the front of their writing folders or portfolios. Getting continuous updates from students makes it easy for you to keep track of who's where in the writing process. It helps students stay on track, too, as they move through various stages with their writing.

Charlotte Sassman
Alice Carlson Applied
Learning Center
Fort Worth, Texas

Literature LINK

From Pictures to Words: A Book About Making a Book

by Janet Stevens (Holiday House, 1995)

The title sounds a bit dry, but this is one hilarious picture book. Janet Stevens, an illustrator (and author of the book), is challenged by some characters from her vivid imagination to take a shot at actually writing a book (usually she just illustrates them). These characters are very insistent and very funny. With their help, Janet writes and illustrates a book and takes readers through the process with a smile. An interesting touch is that Janet renders herself in black and white, while the crazy characters are full of color. The book is lots of fun and informative at the same time.

That's It?! That's All?!

Many students are intimidated by writing because of all the wonderful books they've read. They figure they could never write something as clever or interesting as the authors they read. Help them learn that they can, with this simple activity.

First, make two points with students. One—everyone has stories to tell. Two—it's rarely the ideas that are so brilliant and original, it's the writing. As an example, read aloud a story such as the Newbery Award–winning *Shiloh*, by Phyllis Reynolds Naylor (Atheneum, 1991). This is a universally acclaimed book. Analyze the story in the simplest terms. List what happens on the board. It might look something like this:

- A boy finds a dog.
- The boy keeps the dog.
- The owner wants the dog back.
- The boy makes a deal with the owner to earn the dog.
- The owner gives the boy the dog.

That's it. Is that worth reading about? That's really all that happens, but it's a great story because of the way it is written. As you read stories aloud during the year, repeat this exercise periodically. After students see how simple the story line really is, have them look at and identify the elements of story writing that make the story come alive. This is an exercise that can help students build confidence in themselves as writers and become focused on techniques of good writing that they can incorporate in their own work.

Setting Concentration

Math games. Spelling games. Writing games? Sure. This one lets students explore settings as general as "the jungle" and as specific as "my room."

- Give each student two large index cards. On one card, have students write the name of a setting. This could be something very familiar, such as the classroom or playroom, or something less known, such as the planet Mars. On the other card, have students write a short description of the setting, using as much sensory and informational detail as possible. Limit students to five lines on their descriptions.

- When students finish their cards, collect and shuffle them, then place them facedown.

- Divide the class into two teams and play concentration with the cards. Have one team start by turning over two cards, reading them aloud, and deciding if they match. If the cards match, the team keeps the cards. If the cards don't match, they are turned facedown and the other team takes a turn. Play continues until all cards have been matched.

Literature LINK

Do Not Open

by Brinton Turkle (Dutton, 1981)

One element closely related to setting, and arguably even part of it, is mood. In Brinton Turkle's wonderful *Do Not Open*, the mood is ominous and stormy, with a sense of impending danger. The remote cottage, the stormy sea, the threatening weather—all contribute to the mood. Use the book to examine with students how mood is established through setting and choice of words as well as character. Now try writing some "Moody Paragraphs." Have students write a paragraph that they feel sets a mood. Have students share their paragraphs with a partner to see if the mood is communicated effectively. Encourage students to discuss the ways they used setting and words to create mood.

TIP

A great finished writing product is its own reward, but kids still love that little extra recognition. As students submit pieces that show mastery of a new skill or ability, such as a great setting, super use of descriptive language, or just completion of a challenging piece, give them a "You've Got the Write Stuff!" certificate. (See page 89.) Children will appreciate the extra attention to their writing efforts!

Sound and Setting

Setting is an important part of any story. Have students utilize sound to experiment with setting in their writing.

Play a recording of a sound, such as rain, or make a sound for students, such as the beating of a drum or the impatient tapping of a pencil. Explain to students that you would like them to begin a story with this sound. Start by letting students suggest ways to "spell" the sound. Sometimes a simple "tap, tap, tap" will do. Other times students will need to be more creative, coming up with their own spellings to let readers "hear" the specific sound in their minds. Let students share their stories and compare the directions they took. It's interesting to see that even though all of their stories begin with the same sound and opening, they almost always develop differently. Students will discover that using sound can help set all sorts of moods for a story and make for fun and unusual beginnings that draw readers right in.

ENGLISH Language LEARNERS

Have you ever taken a good look at newspaper headlines? Idioms abound. Many children, particularly those with limited exposure and experience with English, find idioms confusing. To help, bring in newspapers and look at headlines together. Discuss what they mean. Use a good reference like the *Scholastic Dictionary of Idioms*, by Marvin Terban (Scholastic, 1996), as a resource. This book lists idioms alphabetically, gives an example, tells the meaning in clear, child-friendly language, and then provides a short origin, which makes it all the more interesting. After collecting some idioms and going over them in this way, have students try to write a short news article and an accompanying headline that makes use of an idiom.

Senses Web

A big part of helping readers understand what's happening in a story is the use of language that evokes sensory images about characters, setting, and so on. Try this activity to help your young writers connect with the senses as their own stories unfold.

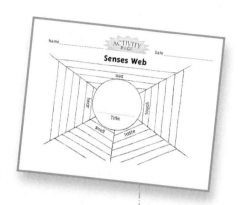

- Give students a copy of the Senses Web graphic organizer. (See page 90.) Review the senses listed. Then use a piece of literature to model how an author creates sensory images with words. For example, share the sample passage from *A Chair for My Mother* (See right.) Ask: "Can you see the blue tile of the diner? Feel the wet cloth washing the salt and pepper shakers? Smell the onions (and maybe even taste that soup)? Hear the jingle of coins going in the jar?"

- Divide the class into small groups, and let each choose a story to analyze for sensory images. Have students find words or passages from the story that engage their senses and record them on their webs.

- Let each group take a turn at the overhead, sharing the webs they created. Provide students with additional copies of the web to complete as they brainstorm their own stories independently.

Literature LINK

Faith and the Electric Dogs

by Patrick Jennings (Scholastic, 1996)

This is a great read-aloud for teaching point of view in writing. Faith is a young girl who befriends a trilingual (Spanish, English, and Dog) street dog, Eddie. After reading the story, have students look through books to identify examples of various points of view. Ask students to consider how a story might be different if told from the point of view of a different character. If Faith were telling the story instead of Eddie, what things might we not know?

"My mother works as a waitress in the Blue Tile Diner. After school sometimes I go to meet her there. Then her boss Josephine gives me a job too. I wash the salts and peppers and fill the ketchups. One time I peeled all the onions for the onion soup. When I finish, Josephine says, 'Good work, honey,' and pays me. And every time, I put half of my money into the jar."

from *A Chair for My Mother* by Vera B. Williams (Greenwillow, 1982)

Spin-a-Story Board Game

This story-building board game for two to four players builds awareness of elements of literature as students create fun-to-share stories.

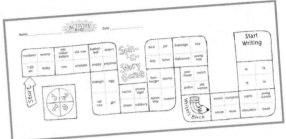

A good reference for further exploration of synonyms is the *Scholastic Dictionary of Synonyms, Antonyms, and Homonyms* (Scholastic, 2001).

⊚ Gather the following materials for each set of players: the game board (see pages 91–92: tape A to B to make the game board), a paper clip, a pencil, blank paper, and a token (such as a bead or small eraser for each player).

⊚ To play, students take turns spinning the spinner (placing a paper clip in the center, then holding a pencil point on the dot and spinning the paper clip) and moving that number of spaces.

⊚ If players land on a space with four boxes, they read the word in each box, then place their marker in one of the boxes and record the word. Each of the words represents a story element—for example, characters (old man, puppy, doctor), settings (ocean, castle, Halloween), and other objects (egg, pajamas, computer). As players spin and move around the board, they accumulate more and more of these story ideas. If a player lands on a Writer's Block space, no word is collected.

⊚ Players take turns in this manner, moving around the board and collecting and writing down words along the way. The game ends for a player when he or she lands on the Start Writing space. By this point players will have collected a number of words. Players then use each word in a short story.

Synonym Pass

Sometimes it's difficult to find "just the right word." Exposure to a rich vocabulary through listening and reading is key to learning the possibilities that are out there, but you can help focus and expand on this vocabulary with a game of Synonym Pass.

⊚ Divide the class into groups of three or four students each and separate them around the room. Write a target word on a sheet of paper. Begin with something simple like the word *big*.

- Share the word with students and tell them they have three minutes in their groups to record as many synonyms for the word as they can.

- At the end of three minutes, pass to one group the sheet of paper on which you've written the target word. Have this group choose a synonym from their list, say it aloud, and add it to the paper.

- This group then passes the paper to the next group. This group must offer another synonym for *big* and record it on the paper. The passing continues until all possibilities from students' lists have been exhausted. Select a new target word and play again!

Essential Editing Checklist

Students (and teachers) appreciate having a checklist to guide the editing process. You can use the one on page 93 as a good example or as a guide for developing your own.

Before sharing the checklist, ask students to name some things they look for when they edit a piece of writing. Reinforce the concept that the reasons we edit for things like punctuation, spelling, and clarity of ideas is to make sure we are communicating clearly and making sense to the reader. Talk about ways students can do each of these things—for example, by reading the piece aloud and noticing if end punctuation appears in logical places. Give students copies of the editing checklist on page 93. Place a writing sample on the overhead and demonstrate how to use the checklist. There's space for the student, a peer editor, and the teacher to check off various parts of the editing process and to make comments.

Wendy Weiner
The Parkview School
Milwaukee, Wisconsin

Give children copies of the "handy" five-step graphic organizer to guide their editing. (See page 94.) Each finger on the drawing of the hand features an editing reminder, such as "check spelling" or "check capital letters."

Adapted from *The Reading-Writing Workshop: Getting Started* by Norma Jackson and Paula Pillow (Scholastic, 1992).

Two Ways of Reading

We often find ourselves reminding students to self-edit, but we need to be sure to help them read critically so that they are able to. This can be very useful when students are writing during tests, particularly those that assess their writing abilities.

Help students learn to read their own writing critically by teaching them to read it in two ways. The first time through, have students read their writing almost aloud in their minds. Does the piece makes sense? Does it flow? Is it understandable and clear? On the second read-through, have students focus on the conventions of the writing. Is punctuation correct? Do sentences start with capital letters? Which words might not be spelled correctly? Reading the piece both ways in separate passes ensures a more complete edit and a better overall product.

Inspiring Polished Pieces

One way to motivate children to prepare a story or poem for a good final copy is to encourage them to enter a writing or poetry contest.

To help students set publishing goals, create a display space for posting contest news. Highlight important information, such as deadlines and requirements. *The Ultimate Guide to Student Contests: Grades K–6,* by Scott Pendleton (Walker, 1998), includes fiction and poetry contests. Sponsors of contests in this book include Children's Television Workshop, the National PTA, and Consumers Union.

Ruth Melendez
High Plains Elementary School
Colorado Springs, Colorado

Collage Covers

Have students choose a story, poem, or report they would like to bring to a final published version and use a popular artistic technique to create a special cover.

- Display some favorite picture books on the chalkboard ledge. Let students tell what appeals to them about each. Focus on how the art on a cover can help draw readers to a book and even communicate key elements of a story.

- Ask students to think about the piece of writing they've selected. What key elements might work on a cover? Provide students with various art materials (markers, crayons, colored pencils, scrap paper, glue, scissors) and a heavy cover stock such as posterboard.

- Introduce collage, perhaps sharing books by Eric Carle as an example, and invite students to use this technique to create covers for their story. They can use tissue paper as Eric Carle does, or combine illustrations, photos, and pictures cut from newspapers or magazines. Small objects work well, too. Remind children to keep their key elements in mind as they select their collage components. Their covers will then give readers a hint at what's inside. What an enticement to open it up and read!

Refrigerator Writers

You see them all the time by the curb on trash pickup days—refrigerator doors! For a creative way to give students' writing an audience, try this unique and motivating display.

Securely bolt an old refrigerator door to a wall. (One outside the classroom will be popular with passersby.) Invite students to submit their best writing for display on the refrigerator door. Display "refrigerator worthy" samples with colorful magnets. This is a good opportunity to provide a public venue for young writers and add a homey touch to the classroom, too.

TIP

A refrigerator door display outside the principal's office (and managed by the principal and/or a student helper) is a great way to get administrators involved in the writing process as they build relationships with students.

Name _____ Date _____

Spooky Story Organizer

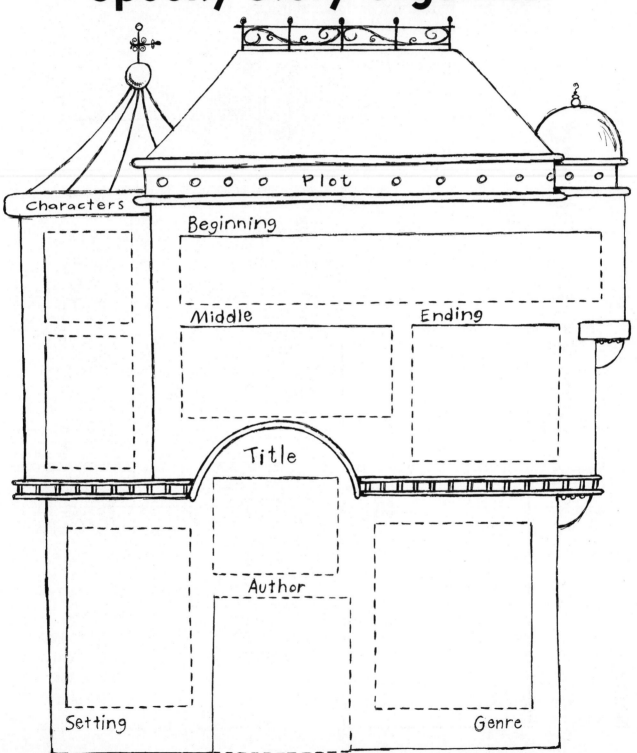

Super Story Board

Name _____ Date _____

A Character Is Born

Goals

_____

_____

Something My
Character Might Say

_____

Born

Year _____

Where _____

What's in My
Character's
Pockets

_____

_____

_____

_____

_____

Important
to Know!

_____

_____

_____

_____

_____

Name of Character

Likes

Dislikes

The Great Big Idea Book: Language Arts © 2009, Scholastic Teaching Resources

Name _____ Date _____

Buddy Interview Outline

Interview Buddy _____

Interview Notes

Age _____ Birthday _____ Birthplace _____

Family Information _____

Hobbies and Activities _____

_____

Pets _____

Favorite Things _____

_____

More Information _____

_____

_____

Closing Statement _____

_____

Name _____ Date _____

Just Write!

"What to write?" I asked my teacher,
That's how I described my plight.

She waved her arms about her,
She fixed me in her sight.

"Write of the soaring, gymnastic hawk slicing through the air.
A flight!" she said. "Just write!"

"Of cheese, tomato, and lettuce. Grilled, tasty, juicy, hot, delicious!
A bite!" she said. "Just write!"

"Of ancient armor, swords at ready, fearsome combat. Courage, bravery!
A knight!" she said. "Just write!"

"Of the slithering, silky, eerie, icy touch of a ghost. Graveyards. Full moon!
A fright!" she said. "Just write!"

And then an idea landed.
Softly, like a kite.
I ran to my desk, grabbed my pencil.
I've got it! This is it.
"Just right!"

—Bob Krech

TAKE-HOME ACTIVITY

Name ______________________ Date ______________

Recipe Writers

Recipe Title ______________________________________

Source ______________________________________

What You Need ______________________________

____

Kitchen Equipment ______________________________

____

____

Directions ______________________________

____

____

____

Written by ______________________

Name _____ Date _____

What a Time We Had Together!

Dear Family,

Congratulations! It's your turn to get the What a Time We Had Together! take-home writing pack. Along with this letter, you'll find two pencils and some writing paper. You and your child will have a chance to talk, plan, write, and read together.

Begin by brainstorming. Think about and discuss a special time you've shared together. It might be a trip, a holiday, a birthday party, or a visit to someone special. It could even be something simple done around the house, such as playing a game or having a yard sale. Decide together on one event you both enjoyed and would like to write about.

Together, jot down some details about that special time. What was it you did? Who was there? What were you wearing? What was the weather like? How were you feeling? What was said? Why is it worth writing about?

Now for the writing. Use the notes for each of you to write a story about the special time. When you are both ready, read your work aloud to each other. Trade pieces and help each other as editors. When your editing is complete, you can each write a final copy on another sheet of paper. Have your child return his or her story to school, along with the materials in the bag. Enjoy, and thanks for participating!

Sincerely,

_____
Your Child's Teacher

The Great Big Idea Book: Language Arts © 2009, Scholastic Teaching Resources

Name _____   Date _____

You Know Me at Home, but . . .

I like to read about

I like to write about

My favorite thing in school is _____

because _____ .

In class I like to _____ .

For lunch I enjoy _____ .

At recess I usually _____ .

Some of my friends in class are _____ .

Something new for me in school this year is _____ .

My name is ⌐ ¬ Fold
            └ ┘ cut

The Great Big Idea Book: Language Arts © 2009, Scholastic Teaching Resources

Name _____

Date _____

Writing Workshop Record

Date	Title of Writing Piece	Activity/Status	Comments

Possible Activities:

Brainstorming	Conferencing	Research Reading	Rough Draft
Editing	Final Draft	Publishing	Illustrating
Cover Art	Peer Editing	Writing	Webbing

You've Got the Write Stuff

Student's Name

You've Got the Write Stuff!

awarded for

Signed _____

Date _____

ACTIVITY **PAGE**

Senses Web

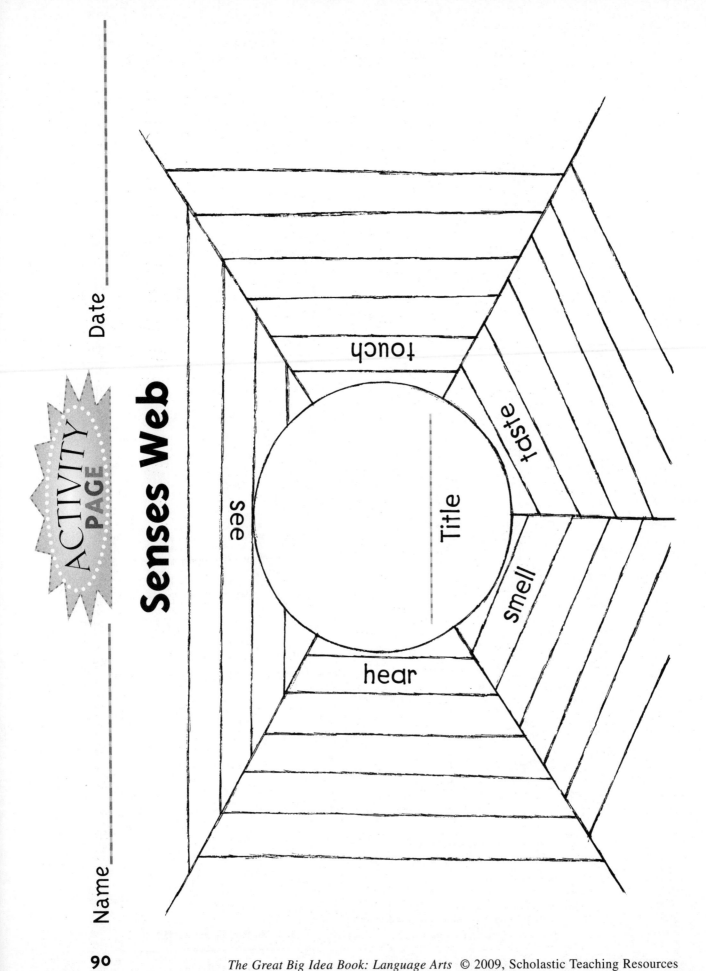

see

touch

taste

Title

smell

hear

The Great Big Idea Book: Language Arts © 2009, Scholastic Teaching Resources

ACTIVITY **PAGE**

Spin-a-Story Game

stormy night	cactus
dinner robbery	

A

desert	basket-ball	old man	one million dollars	swamp	root beer
pajamas	puppy	airplane	zoo	baby	7:00 am

egg	midnight
girl	tall tree

Start

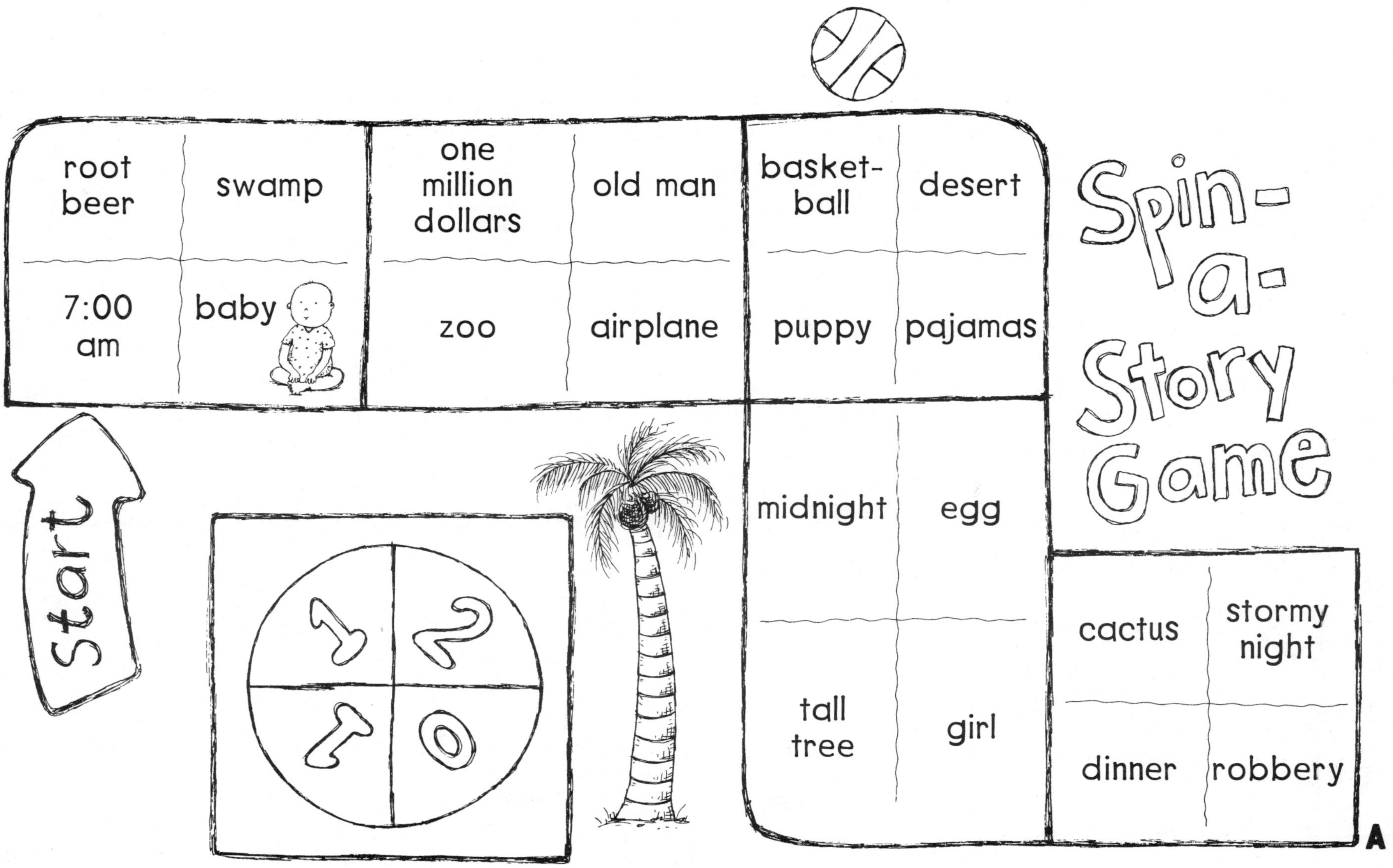

Start Writing

car	picnic	
snow	dragon	
young woman	castle	
book	chocolate	

shovel computer	
ocean	noon

key	bandage
young man	Halloween

watch	your house
old woman	police

Writer's Block

bird	jail
boy	letter

doctor	ham- burger
museum	space- ship

The Great Big Idea Book: Language Arts © 2009, Scholastic Teaching Resources   **B**

Name _____ Date _____

Essential Editing Checklist

Idea	Self-Edit	Peer Editor/Comments	Teacher Editor/Comments
Makes Sense			
Spelling			
Punctuation			
Capitalization			
Ending Punctuation			
Beginning			
Ending			
Story Elements			

Name _____   Date _____

Five-Step Editing

Use one of these to end a sentence:

. ? !

Start a sentence with a capital letter.

Write names of people, places, and pets with a capital letter.

Check spelling.

Space between words.

Revising and Editing Marks

Take something away

Add something

Check spelling

Capitalize

Indent the paragraph

Grammar

Whoever heard of having fun learning the rules of language? Well, with games like Beanillionaire and Punctuation Bounce, your students will be eager to master the skills that lead to correct writing and speaking. This section features both of these games (see pages 119 and 121), along with dozens of other activities and tips that will enliven grammar lessons and motivate students to learn punctuation, mechanics, sentence structure, and more. The activities in this section are designed to help students grow in confidence and skill as writers and speakers.

To support your instructional goals, the activities are aligned with the MCREL standards, which suggest that students in grades 2 and 3 use the following grammatical conventions in their writing: various sentence types; nouns, verbs, adjectives, and adverbs; and conventions of capitalization and punctuation.

This section can help you provide instruction in those areas through activities that connect with other curriculum areas and tap into the many ways students learn. For example, Adjective Detectives puts a scientific spin on language lessons as students use attributes to try to identify the hidden object in a sock. (See page 102.) In Noun Walk-Around, students explore parts of speech in the world around them. (See page 100.) And in Punctuation Bounce, a ball gives students a hands-on lesson in using end punctuation and capital letters. (See page 121.)

What's My Noun?

This guessing game gets children writing and guessing as they identify nouns by examining attributes.

- Write "What's My Noun?" at the top of a sheet of chart paper or a white board. Cut a slit in the top of a shoe box and place it next to the display.

- Write various nouns on slips of paper and place the papers in a bag. Or, for a more concrete version, place actual objects in a bag.

- Invite a child to choose a noun from the bag and then describe it (without naming it) on the chart paper or white board. For example, the child might describe the noun's shape, color, and size, and tell what it's used for.

- Have students guess the noun, write it on a slip of paper, and place it in the box. At a designated time, let the child who created the list read students' guesses and reveal the noun.

- Repeat daily to give additional children a chance to describe nouns for the class and to let students become more skilled at identifying specific nouns—for example, basketball instead of ball.

Maryanne Frawley
Amery, Wisconsin

TIP

For a partner version of this activity, let children choose a noun to describe. Then pair up children and let them make and trade lists of words that describe their "secret" nouns. Can they guess each other's nouns?

Literature LINK

A Mink, a Fink, a Skating Rink: What Is a Noun?

by Brian P. Cleary (Carolrhoda Books, 2000)

"Hill is a noun. Mill is a noun. Even Uncle Phil is a noun." Rhyming text and lively illustrations zip readers along in this out-of-the-ordinary lesson on nouns. Children will have fun substituting their own words for those in the book to learn more about nouns and make new rhymes.

Rhyming People, Places, Things

Let children draw inspiration from Brian Cleary's *A Mink, a Fink, a Skating Rink: What Is a Noun?* to create their own sets of rhyming nouns. The wordplay is pure fun, but students will get plenty of practice with word choice, too.

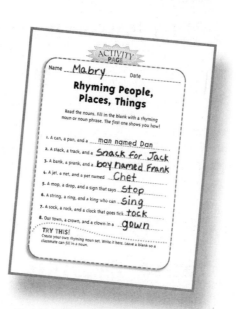

fter sharing the book, invite students to brainstorm nouns that rhyme. How about a *home*, a *dome*, and a *gnome* from *Rome*? After sharing some ideas, give students copies of page 124. Have them complete each set of rhyming nouns by filling in the blanks. Then invite them to make up their own sets of rhyming nouns. A rhyming dictionary will come in handy and help broaden students' thinking about their word choices. (See Tip, right.) Have students choose three or more rhyming nouns and then write their words on drawing paper and add illustrations. Put the pages together to make a book, or use them to collaborate on creating a colorful banner that wraps around the room.

Literature LINK

The Letters Are Lost

by Lisa Campbell Ernst (Viking Penguin, 1996)

In a book about lost letters, A is discovered in an airplane and B in a bath. "C joined a family of Cows. D was a Dog's tasty treat." Use the book to highlight nouns. (For each letter of the alphabet, the noun in the sentence is capitalized.) Then get ready for more with the book's ending: The letters are together again but not for long. Can readers guess where they're going?

Find more than 15,000 words in *The Scholastic Rhyming Dictionary*, by Sue Young (Scholastic, 1994), a kid-friendly resource organized by vowel sounds and final syllables.

Letters on the Move

Students write a sequel to a clever alphabet book to put a playful twist on what they know about parts of speech.

Share *The Letters Are Lost.* (See page 97.) After reading the ending, let students guess where the letters are off to now. Write each letter of the alphabet on a slip of paper and place the papers in a bag. Have children randomly choose a letter to write about in an innovation on the book. Students can use the book as a model for sentence structure and illustration (block-style-alphabet).

Take-Home Activity:
Noun-a-Morphs

Children learn that nouns name people, places, and things, but things get tricky when it comes to capitalization. Try this "morphing" activity to have fun learning the difference between common nouns and proper nouns.

⑤ Invite children to share what they know about nouns. Let them look around the room and take turns naming some nouns. Help students recognize that nouns name people, places, and things.

⑤ Review what students know about using capital letters. If you use a morning message, have students identify words with capital letters and the kinds of nouns these words name. For example, the date names a thing, your signature names a person, and so on. (Note that using the morning message in this way is also an opportunity to point out other instances in which capital letters are used, including in greetings such as "Good Morning, Boys and Girls.")

⑤ Give each child a copy of page 125. Ask children to share what they know about morphing, then explain that you want them to morph all the words in the first column to make them proper nouns. Read through the words in the first column together, and review what they have in common. (They're all nouns. They don't have capital letters.)

⑤ Let children take home the pages and let their families help them morph each noun to make a proper noun. When children return their papers to school, let them take turns sharing the words they chose and the letters they capitalized.

Children may have an easier time identifying nouns that are concrete, such as *child* or *school.* Help children recognize that sometimes a noun can also name a thing that is more abstract, such as friendship or excitement.

Word-Building Inventions

This adventurous activity lets students put nouns together to design inventions.

Work with students to create a list of nouns on the board. Challenge students to put two or more words together to invent something new—for example, someone might put *sky* and *bicycle* together to create a *skycycle*, a bike that is ridden in the sky instead of on the ground. Invite students to sketch a design of their invention and describe in writing its purpose and benefits. Provide time for sharing and comments.

Jacqueline Clarke
Cicero Elementary
Cicero, New York

Nouns for Math Practice

Connect math and grammar by letting students add nouns to their math word problems.

Lots of math worksheets have word problems that involve somebody doing something. Somebody has apples to divide evenly among friends; somebody has money to buy candy and needs to know how much is left over; somebody wants to save money for something and needs to know how long it will take . . . . Problems like these are perfect for reinforcing parts of speech—in particular, nouns. Use a correction pen to white out any names, places, or things in the word problem. Let students read the problem and fill in words that make sense. They'll get practice capitalizing proper nouns and using context to figure out where names for people, places, and things belong.

Noun Walk-Around

This game lets students enjoy a walk outside as they notice and name nouns.

- Review the definition of a noun, then brainstorm a chartful of them. Ask students which of those nouns they might find on a walk around the school.

- Give each student a small paper bag to take on a walk. It will be helpful for students to bring notepads or clipboards and pencils.

- As they take their walk, have students notice objects around them—for example, tiny stones, leaves on the ground, small sticks, and pinecones. Before they put the objects in their bags, have them jot down a note about where they found it—for example, on the ground next to a tree.

- Back inside, have students take turns sharing their nouns. Spread out a large sheet of mural paper, and let students work together to create a mini-version of their walk. Have them glue their objects to the paper, then add details such as trees, leaves, and paths.

- To reinforce vocabulary, have students label the nouns in their mural. They can continue to add labels as they notice and name additional details in their artwork.

For a challenge, add a rule: Students can use up to but no more than three nouns from the same category— for example, no more than three names, three animals, or three fruits.

Alphabet Countdown

After studying nouns for a few days, try this timed activity to have some fun with nouns students know.

Give each student a copy of the record sheet on page 126. Ask children how many nouns they think they can name in three minutes (one for each letter of the alphabet). Let them make their guesses, then start the timer. At the end of three minutes, let students pair up and exchange papers. Have them put a star next to words they think are nouns and circle those they don't think are nouns. Have students take back their own papers and count the number of words that are nouns. If students can use as nouns any of the circled words on their papers, award extra credit. Repeat the activity another day. Can students increase the number of nouns they name in three minutes?

Cynthia Faughnan
Hartford Memorial Middle School
White River Junction, Vermont

Pronoun Bingo

Children put pronouns in their place with this variation on Bingo.

On slips of paper, write sentences that contain pronouns. Include subject (*I, you, he, she, it, we, you, they*), object (*me, you, him, her, it, us, you, them*), and possessive (*my, your, his, her, its, our, their, mine, yours, his, hers, its, ours, theirs*) pronouns. Give each child a copy of the Bingo board on page 127 and a handful of markers (such as dried beans). Write pronouns from the sentences on the board and have children copy the words on their boards, one word per square. Randomly select a sentence from the bag and read it aloud, leaving out a pronoun (inserting a pause in place of it). Have children listen carefully and decide if they have a pronoun that fits. If they have this word, have them put a marker on the square. Play until someone has five squares filled in across, down, or diagonally.

Advertising Adjectives

Students learn about words that describe nouns with an activity that also reinforces consumer skills.

⑤ Invite students to bring in and share advertisements for favorite products—for example, food they like, games, and sneakers. If possible, tape a few commercials to view with students, too.

⑤ Ask what all the materials have in common. Guide students to recognize that the ads try to get a person to buy something. Ask how the ads do it (by describing the product with lots of favorable words). Explain that the describing words advertisers use are called adjectives. They tell more about the product (a noun).

⑤ Have students identify adjectives from the ads. List them on chart paper. Help students see that adjectives tell what kind, which one, or how many.

⑤ Let students develop their talent in this field of writing by creating their own ads (or commercials) to sell a favorite toy or other product. (Students might like to work in groups for this.) Have them write an ad for the product and underline all the adjectives they use. Students can display print ads or perform commercials.

Janet Worthington-Samo
St. Clement School
Johnstown, Pennsylvania

Adjective Detectives

Students focus on word choice while stretching science skills with this interactive display.

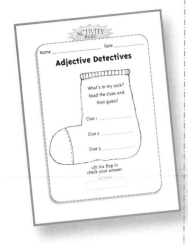

Have students bring in odd socks. Tack the socks to a bulletin board, making sure there's one for each child, then have students choose a small object to hide in their socks. Give them all a chance to place the object in the sock without anyone looking. Make copies of the Adjective Detectives form on page 128 and give one to each child. Have children complete the form, writing three descriptive clues about the object in their sock (such as size, shape, and color) and then filling in the name of the object in the space provided. Show students how to make a flap to cover the name of the object by cutting a small piece of paper to size, placing it over the name, then taping only the top edge. Let students visit the bulletin board to guess their classmates' mystery objects. They can lift the flaps to self-check.

Paula W. Hotard
St. Philomena School
Labadieville, Louisiana

Literature LINK

Juba This and Juba That

by Virginia Tashjian (Little, Brown, 1995)

This playful collection of stories, songs, chants, poems, rhymes, and riddles includes the irresistible "What Did You Put in Your Pocket?" by Beatrice Schenk de Regniers. The poem begins "What did you put in your pocket/What did you put in your pocket/in your pockety pockety pocket/Early Monday morning?" The verse repeats for each day of the week, with an answer after each that ranges from "slushy glushy pudding" on Monday to a "spinky spanky handkerchief" on Sunday. The refrain cumulatively repeats what's in the pocket for each day of the week, so by the end students will be chiming in with a long list. For an innovation on the poem that strengthens the use of adjectives, let students take turns substituting something new for each day of the week.

Interactive Morning Message:
I Spy Adjectives

The detail-packed I Spy books are perfect for exploring adjectives. This morning message lets children go further by writing their own mini I Spy adjective riddles.

Share *I Spy Super Challenger*. (See below.) As children solve the riddles, take time to identify adjectives. Guide children to notice numbers that tell how many (*two* snowmen), words that tell what color (a *brown-and-white* dog), words that describe sizes (*little* glass heart), and so on. Display a picture from the book, along with a morning message that invites children to describe something they "spy." Have children write their mini I Spy riddles on the morning message and sign their names. Take time at your morning meeting to let children solve their classmates' riddles. Repeat the activity with other scenes from the book.

Literature
LINK

I Spy Super Challenger

by Jean Marzollo and Walter Wick (Scholastic, 1997)

I Spy fans will recognize favorite pictures from previous I Spy books, each with an all-new riddle. The scenes in this collection are among the most complex, and the new riddles that go with them challenge children to find some of the most difficult details—including plenty of objects to reinforce lessons on adjectives. "A little blue duck," "six red shoes," "ballet slippers," "a birthday candle," and "chocolate sauce" are just a few of the examples students come across in their I Spy adventures.

Adjective Olympics

Which student has the longest feet? Who can tell the funniest joke? Who's the fastest runner? Who's wearing the most colorful socks? Who has the strangest pet? Your students will make all sorts of interesting discoveries about their classmates with this Olympic activity.

- Make copies of the Adjective Olympics medal on page 129.

- Brainstorm with students adjectives that could describe something special about their classmates. These can be silly, strange, or serious (but always positive).

- Let students suggest a winner for first place in each category. Then, let each student complete and decorate a medal for another child; then hold an awards ceremony. Play some majestic music before bringing students up one at a time to accept their medals.

Adapted from *25 Great Grammar Poems With Activities,* by Bobbi Katz (Scholastic, 1999).

Literature LINK

Hairy, Scary, Ordinary: What Is an Adjective?

by Brian P. Cleary (Carolrhoda, 2000)

"They're colorful, like mauve and puce. They help explain, like lean and loose." Playful rhymes and whimsical illustrations whisk readers from page to page to learn about adjectives. As an extension, reread the book and let students add on to each type of adjective that is introduced—for example, adjectives that describe or explain.

I'm an Adjective! Mini-Thesaurus

This mini-thesaurus get students using reference books as they explore descriptive vocabulary.

Give each student a copy of page 130. Have students fold the pages to make a book. Invite children to think of adjectives that describe them, then record them on pages 2–4 in the space provided. As a lesson in using a thesaurus, have students find and list synonyms for each adjective. To follow up, you might invite students to write descriptive paragraphs about each other, using the words in the mini-thesaurus.

Colorful Caterpillars Grow Long

This interactive display invites children to explore adjectives and adverbs as they create long, colorful caterpillars.

- Make two copies of the caterpillar face pattern on page 131. Enlist children's help in cutting out additional ovals from construction paper.

- After sharing a book with children, revisit a few sentences to identify adjectives and adverbs. Let children name other adjectives and adverbs on their own. Record some of their words on the ovals (one per oval). Gather students outside the classroom and put up the start of the caterpillar displays—tacking up one caterpillar "face" and adding on adjective ovals, then doing the same for the adverbs with the second caterpillar face. Add construction paper legs, two per oval. Reread the words with children.

- Continue to add to each caterpillar as students identify more adjectives and adverbs in books they read. Can students make their caterpillars stretch down the hall and around the corner? Passersby will enjoy seeing all the words and learning some colorful word choices for their writing.

Wendy Weiner
Parkview Elementary School
Milwaukee, Wisconsin

The *Scholastic Children's Thesaurus*, by John K. Bollard (Scholastic, 1998), defines synonyms. Illustrations provide visual clues and information boxes invite children to learn more.

Adjectives About Me

Students create self-portraits with words, learning more about themselves and becoming more skilled at choosing and using specific language.

After teaching adjectives, ask children to name adjectives that describe themselves and/or each other. Record suggestions on chart paper and display them. Encourage children to be specific in their choices. Although *nice* might fit, stronger choices might be *helpful* and *cheerful*. Give children copies of page 132. Have children complete each section to describe themselves, then write their name at the bottom and make a paper flap to cover it.

Lyn MacBruce
Randolph Elementary School
Randolph, Vermont

ENGLISH Language LEARNERS

Cutting out pictures from magazines gives English language learners a chance to learn language skills through multiple approaches—in this case, the activity provides a learning experience that is both visual and hands-on. Start by giving students a list of adjectives. Have them look for and cut out pictures that represent these words and then use them to create a collage. Have students copy the adjectives from the list on sticky notes and use them to label the adjectives in the picture. They can remove the words and repeat this part of the activity (and do the same with classmates' collages) to expand their vocabulary for and understanding of adjectives. For a more basic approach to this activity, start with an adjective such as *red*. Have children find pictures of things that are red and cut them out for their collages.

Dunk, Dive, Slide!

Students make a web of sports verbs to practice using specific language to describe actions.

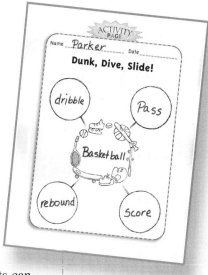

Take students outside or to another open space to play a game such as kickball or soccer. After they've had plenty of action, bring them back to the classroom for some wordplay. Draw a large web on the board. Write the name of the game in the center. Invite students to suggest action words that describe the game. Record these words on the web. If students suggest words that are related to the game but are not verbs, guide them to make another choice. As a follow-up, give students copies of the web template on page 133. Let them make a web of action words that describe a favorite sport. (Students can draw inspiration from the sports pages, too.) Display webs on a bulletin board decorated with pictures of balls and other sports equipment.

Wendy Wise-Borg
Rider University
Lawrenceville, New Jersey

Literature LINK

To Root, to Toot, to Parachute: What Is a Verb?

by Brian P. Cleary (Carolrhoda, 2001)

"Verbs are words like sing and dance, pray or practice, preach or prance, toss and tumble, jump and jam, whine and whisper, sleep and slam." This fast-paced book introduces action words (along with other kinds of verbs), and will lead to lots of fun follow-up activities. For example, have students add to the list of verbs above, suggesting pairs of verbs that use alliterative language. How about *leap* and *look, bake* and *beep, read* and *ride, swim* and *sweep*?

TIP

For a variation on the sports words web, invite students to think of a favorite activity. Have them write about it on a sentence strip, using verbs to tell about the action. Then invite them to draw pictures of themselves doing the activity.

Take-Home Activity:
Clap, Wiggle, Stomp

The familiar and favorite song "If You're Happy and You Know It" invites students to come up with actions for new verses—which means building their vocabulary of verbs.

🌀 Write the words to "If You're Happy and You Know It" on chart paper:

> If you're happy and you know it, clap your hands,
>
> If you're happy and you know it, clap your hands,
>
> If you're happy and you know it, then the whole wide world should know it,
>
> If you're happy and you know it, clap your hands.

🌀 Ask students what the action is in the song. (*clapping*) Underline the word *clap* each time it appears. Then sing the song together and let children join in on the action.

🌀 Since one time through won't be enough, ask children what other verbs (or actions) they could substitute for *clap*. List their ideas— for example, *stomp your feet, wave your hands, touch your toes,* and *jump up high*—and then sing the new verses.

🌀 Let children share their action-packed song at home. Give them copies of page 134. In the spaces provided, have students fill in the verbs (or verb phrases) for new verses. Can they and their family members think of other actions? Take time to sing them in school.

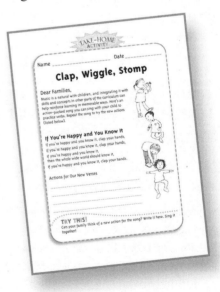

Actions With Impact

This unconventional lesson lets students discover the impact of strong verbs on their writing.

Surprise students in the middle of a fairly calm activity (such as a read-aloud) by acting out an unexpected and lively scenario— for example, you might pretend you saw a spaceship go by the classroom window or act very bothered by a nonexistent fly that won't leave you alone (stomp around it, swat at it, wave it away). Act out the scenario as dramatically as you can in order to give children lots of material to describe later on.

After your theatrical experience, explain that it was just an act, then invite children to describe what they heard and saw. Record their comments on the board. ("You jumped from your seat and rushed to the window; you shouted for us to come, too; you pointed to the sky; you shrieked that there was a spaceship," and so on.)

After soliciting a dozen sentences, have students identify the verbs in each. Then write as nondescriptive a sentence about the event as you can on the board ("I saw a spaceship") and compare it with students' sentences. Guide students to recognize the importance of strong verbs in their writing.

TIP

Follow up by asking students to circle the verbs in a draft they're working on. Challenge them to replace vague or redundant verbs with more descriptive ones. Invite them to notice strong verbs in books they're reading.

ENGLISH Language LEARNERS

Play a lively game of Simon Says to help English language learners develop vocabulary for verbs. Pair up students. Let them take turns giving each other Simon Says commands with one verb—for example, "Simon says, Sit." Build up to two verb commands and then three. Performing the actions named by the verbs will help English language learners remember their meaning. And everyone will enjoy the chance to move!

Action Name Tags

These name tags let students tell something about themselves as they learn more about verbs.

⚙ Have each student choose a verb that starts with the same first letter as his or her name. (*Rob runs, Sara snowboards, Wendy whistles*) If students are new to learning verbs, you may want to post "verb banks" around your classroom that list a variety of verbs for students to choose from. An alternative is to have students each check their choice with you before proceeding, to make sure that they are making correct word choices.

⚙ Give each student a sheet of sturdy paper. Have students fold their papers in half lengthwise to make name tags that will sit on their desks. Let them write their verbs and names on the paper and then illustrate themselves in action.

⚙ When everyone's finished, let students take a walk around the room to appreciate the many action words that describe their classmates. Students will also enjoy using these name tags to point families in the right direction at open-school night.

Maryanne Frawley
Amery, Wisconsin

For a variation on this activity, have students choose an adjective that begins with the first letter of their name and is also descriptive of themselves. Let children create name tags that combine the adjectives and their names.

Fishing for Verbs

This pantomime activity begins with a fish bowl full of verbs.

Write verbs on slips of paper and place them in a fish bowl. Gather children in a circle to form a "pond," and pass the fish bowl to a volunteer. Have this student take a verb from the fish bowl, go to the center of the pond, and act out the word. Have the child who guesses the word take the next turn. Continue until everyone who wants a chance to act out a verb has had one.

When? Where? How?

"The Southwest has never seen a snowstorm like this before." "The game-winning hit was over the fence." "The governor made the announcement unexpectedly." The newspaper is full of adverbs—words that tell when, where, or how something happened. Use newspapers to help children see how these describing words make writing stronger.

⊚ Cut out newspaper stories and highlight adverbs that tell when, where, and how.

⊚ Divide the class into small groups. Give each an article and ask students to read aloud the story. Then decide together what the highlighted words have in common.

⊚ Bring students together to share their words and ideas. Create a three-column chart labeled "When," "Where," and "How." Ask students to record their words in the corresponding columns.

⊚ Discuss how adverbs help make writing stronger. Then let children write a short news story about a school or family event. Encourage them to use adverbs to provide specific information that answers the questions when, where, or how.

Share students' news stories on the back of the weekly note home. You might be able to fit three or four on the back of each note. Over a period of a couple of months, each student will have a chance to share a story in this way.

The -*ly* Walk

Students will enjoy getting from one place to another in school with an activity that lets them act out adverbs.

Brainstorm words that end in -*ly* and tell how—for example, *happily, quickly, quietly, slowly, proudly,* and *casually.* Write these words on slips of paper and place them in a bag. Each day, when it's time to line up and go to lunch, recess, and so on, let a child choose a word and lead the class in moving down the hallway as described by the adverb. Add new words to the bag as students notice -*ly* adverbs in their reading.

Grammar-Gories

Students practice using parts of speech in this variation of a popular game.

London
lake
licked
will look
likable
lazily

ⓢ Write the following categories on the board: Proper Noun, Common Noun, Past-Tense Verb, Future-Tense Verb, Adjective, Adverb.

ⓢ Randomly choose a letter of the alphabet. (See Tip, left.) Demonstrate how to name a word for each category that starts with that letter. If the letter is *l*, you might use the word *London* for proper noun, *lake* for common noun, *licked* for past-tense verb, and so on.

ⓢ Give each student a copy of page 135. Choose another random letter and have children record it on their paper in the appropriate space. Have children write down a word that starts with that letter for each category. The first person to fill in a word for each category calls out "Stop," at which point all students put down their pencils.

ⓢ To award points, the student who finished first reads his or her word for proper noun. If no one else had that word, then everyone who had a word for that category gets one point. If someone else had the same word, no points are awarded. The leader proceeds with words in each additional category and the scoring continues. At the end of the scoring, choose another letter and start a new round. For a cooperative scoring method, give everyone time to record a word for each category. Have students share their words, crossing off any that another student also has. How many different words did students come up with for each category?

Emily A. Olesch
Star of the Sea School
Virginia Beach, Virginia

Here's a fun way to randomly choose a letter of the alphabet: Have a student silently say the alphabet. After a moment, say "Stop." Use whatever letter of the alphabet the child was on as the target letter.

Flipping Over Parts of Speech

Children construct some amusing sentences with a flip book that targets parts of speech.

- ✿ Give each child multiple copies of page 136. Have children cut out the mini-book pages, stack them, and staple them at the top. Guide children in cutting the center dashed line of each page to make flaps.

- ✿ Brainstorm noun phrases with children and write them on the board—for example, "The ice cream," "Our teacher," "The hippopotamus," "The cat," "An alligator," "A boy," and "A girl." Do the same for verb phrases—for example, "won the race," "had the hiccups," "watched cartoons," "rode a roller coaster," "ate biscuits," "caught a mouse," and "suddenly screeched."

- ✿ Have students copy a noun phrase on the left flap of each page. Have them copy a verb phrase on the right flap of each page. Invite students to illustrate each flap.

- ✿ Show students how to flip the sections back and forth to build dozens of silly sentences—for example, with the phrases listed above, they can create these sentences and more: "An alligator ate biscuits." "The ice cream won the race." "The hippopotamus rode a roller coaster."

Karen K. Bjork (retired)
Portage Public Schools
Portage, Michigan

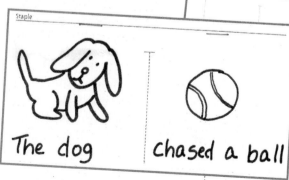

113

Cut-and-Paste Parts of Speech

Don't underestimate the power of a few art supplies, scissors, and a little glue! These simple materials bring life to this parts-of-speech lesson.

Invite students to search in magazines for nouns, verbs, adjectives, or other parts of speech you're studying. Have them cut out the words from headlines, advertisements, and other places where the type tends to be bigger. Let students use the words to form sentences, pasting them in place on construction paper, then adding illustrations. Students won't be able to make as many sentences as on a fill-in worksheet, but they will be much more likely to remember what they learn this way.

Maryanne Frawley
Amery, Wisconsin

Funny Fill-Ins

Mad Libs are a favorite with children. These fill-in-the-blank stories give students lots of practice with parts of speech, with very humorous results. Here's an activity that turns commercial worksheet pages into mini-Mad-Lib-like stories that are just as much fun.

Make a copy of several commercial grammar worksheets that ask children to complete sentences by filling in nouns, verbs, adjectives, adverbs, and so on. Use a correction pen to white out several additional words (nouns, verbs, adjectives, and adverbs) in each sentence—for example, an altered sentence might read _____ (noun that names a person) went to _____ (noun that names a place) to _____ (verb). Photocopy the revised worksheets and give one to each child. Pair up students, making sure each partner has a different sheet. Have students take turns asking their partners to supply the parts of speech called for in each sentence. (Partners should not be told the sentence before they supply the requested words.) Have students read completed sentences aloud for some silly results.

Janice Reutter
Boone, Iowa

Double-Agent Words

Students are often confused by words that have more than one usage—for example, words such as *can* that function both as a noun and a verb. Try this activity to familiarize students with such words and have some fun with wordplay.

- Write the following two sentences on the board: "Open the can of soup." "I can write my name." Ask students to identify the word that appears in both sentences. (*can*)

- Ask students to define the word *can* in each sentence. Guide students to notice that even though *can* looks, sounds, and is spelled the same in each sentence, it means different things. Ask students if *can* is a thing or an action in the first sentence. The second sentence?

- Share a couple of other examples of words that function as both nouns and verbs—for example, *present*, *saw*, and *heat*. Notice words that change pronunciation with use—for example: I got a *present* for my birthday. I will *present* my science project on Tuesday. You must *wind* this clock to make it work. The *wind* blew my hat off.

- Once students have the idea, let them team up to find their own double-agent words. Have students write two sentences. One should use the word as a noun, and the other should use it as a verb. Let students share their sentences, leaving blanks for the double-agent words. Can their classmates guess the word that fits in both sentences? For an extra challenge, invite students to write one sentence that uses the same word as a noun and a verb.

Janet Worthington-Samo
St. Clement School
Johnstown, Pennsylvania

TIP

Make a game of using the dictionary to learn more about words with more than one usage. Challenge teams of students to find a word in the dictionary that has the most ways to use it. You might limit their search to words that start with, for example, the letter *a*. Being aware of multiple usage helps students with spelling, too.

I saw the saw on the workbench.

Movement

Stand-Up Sentences

Students stand up and arrange themselves to make sentences. But they don't stay that way for long. Classmates can replace someone standing if they have the same part of speech!

Write a sentence on a sentence strip and cut it apart, word by word. Distribute the words to volunteers. Ask students to stand with their words and arrange themselves at the front of the room to make a sentence. From here, you can do a number of things. You can distribute other words and have students replace each other in the sentence. For example, ask, "Who could replace Sandy?" If Sandy has a noun, only those students also holding a noun could volunteer to replace her. Read the sentence aloud to see how it changes with the new student. You can also have students add adjectives and other parts of speech to the sentences.

Maryanne Frawley
Amery, Wisconsin

ENGLISH
Language
LEARNERS

In activities that ask students to build sentences with different parts of speech, try color-coding words to help English language learners make choices. For example, write nouns in green, adjectives in purple, and verbs in red. Have students follow color patterns to put words together and build basic sentences—for example, sentences with a simple subject (*The dog*) and simple predicate (*barked*) would always be green and red.

Our Absolutely Awesome Alphabet

This collaborative bookmaking project has children playing with parts of speech from *A* to *Z*.

Share *The Absolutely Awful Alphabet*. (See below.) Then let each student choose a letter to create a class innovation on the book. (Leave the letter *Z* for the class to do together. If you have other letters left over, invite the principal, school nurse, and other members of the staff to contribute a page.) Before students begin writing, revisit various letters in the book and identify adjectives, nouns, verbs, and adverbs on each page. Have students meet with the classmate who has the next letter in the alphabet to create the transition from one letter to the next. Students can add illustrations to their pages, then put them together to make a book.

Literature LINK

The Absolutely Awful Alphabet

by Mordicai Gerstein (Harcourt Brace, 1999)

"A is an awfully arrogant Amphibian annoyed at . . . B who is a bashful, belching Bumpkin bullied by . . ." From *A* to *Z*, this book is full of adjectives, nouns, verbs, adverbs, and other "absolutely awful" parts of speech. Read it to see how choosing the right words can make for writing that paints unforgettable pictures.

Mustn't, Don't, Won't

Use poetry to help students learn more about using contractions in their writing.

Share Shel Silverstein's poem "Listen to the Mustn'ts," from *Where the Sidewalk Ends* (Harper & Row, 1974). Copy it on chart paper and let students highlight the contractions. Then set up a chart for recording the two words that make up the contractions, including, *mustn't, don't, shouldn't,* and *won't*. Let students take turns recording contractions and the two words that make them.

Wendy Wise-Borg
Rider University
Lawrenceville, New Jersey

Animal Cracker Statements

Cooperative groups use animal crackers as springboards to construct declarative sentences.

⑥ Show children an animal cracker and ask them to identify what kind of animal it is. Write the animal's name on the board. (We'll say it's a lion for demonstration purposes.)

⑥ Ask children for information about the lion. ("The lion roars loudly.") Write this on the board. Then ask students to name more things that the lion does. ("The lion hunts. The lion sleeps. The lion eats.") Write these statements on the board, too.

⑥ Explain that a statement tells about something: It's more than one word; it is about one particular person or thing, in this case, a lion. But a statement also tells what that lion does. Invite children to point out the two parts of each sentence (subject and predicate).

⑥ Ask students how they can tell where one sentence ends and another begins. Let them see that statements always begin with a capital letter and end with a period. Now for the fun! Divide the class into groups and give each group a box of animal crackers. Have each group write statements about their animals and illustrate them. Display the sentences and illustrations, and invite students to find the subjects and predicates in each.

Janet Worthington-Samo
St. Clement School
Johnstown, Pennsylvania

Proofreading Like Pros

Proofreading is an obvious way for students to practice grammatical conventions, including punctuation, sentence structure, and word use. This activity challenges them to spot the errors even professional proofreaders missed!

- Explain to students that even though published material, such as a newspaper, gets proofread, mistakes still happen. Locate a newspaper article that contains a grammatical mistake, and place a transparency of it on the overhead. Challenge children to find the mistake.

- Ask children how many grammatical errors in published material they think they can find in one week. Provide the paper for review each day, and encourage children to look at home, too. You can also suggest other sources, such as kids' current events magazines and class or school newsletters.

- Have students highlight the mistakes, write the correction on an index card, and display both on a bulletin board. Take time to let students share their proofreading accomplishments, explaining the error and the correction. Encourage them to apply the same careful proofreading skills to their own work!

Beanillionaire Game

This game, piggybacked off the Millionaire game, means big beans for students who correctly answer grammar questions. Here's how it works.

Put together a set of grammar questions, each with four possible answers. (See sample, right.) Children might like to help come up with questions, too. Divide the class into groups. Explain that each team will be asked a series of questions about grammar and will be given four possible answers. Students on each team will take turns answering the questions. If children aren't sure of the answer, they may ask a buddy for help, ask to have two incorrect answers removed, or take an educated guess. If they answer correctly, they get 100 beans. Try to play the game more than once, having each team keep track of their beans from one round to the next. For more fun, let students use the beans to buy prizes (such as pencils and stickers) in an end-of-the-week auction.

Judy Wetzel
Bull Run Elementary
Centreville, Virginia

Sample Beanillionaire Question

What has the same meaning as *they're*?
a. there
b. their
c. they are
d. they there

If, And, But

This game challenges children to work together to form three-part sentences that use conjunctions.

○ On sentence strips, write sentences that use conjunctions. (Common conjunctions include *and, but, so, or,* and *because.*) Cut each sentence into three parts: the part before the conjunction, the conjunction, and the part after the conjunction. Make sure there is a sentence part for each child.

○ Give each child part of a sentence. Explain that children need to search for two partners to complete their sentence. Because the goal is to have everyone be part of a sentence, children may need to rearrange themselves after forming their sentence in order to make other sentences work.

○ Once everyone has found partners, let children read aloud the sentences. Ask students to tell how each conjunction connects the other two parts.

Connect Two

Children pair up to write sentences on a selected topic, then see how fast they can connect them using conjunctions.

Brainstorm topics that can generate lots of discussion—for example, favorite after-school activities, bedtime, cafeteria food, or homework. Write the topics on slips of paper, then let a volunteer randomly choose one. Ask each child to write a sentence on that topic. When everyone has a sentence, have children pair up and try to join their sentences with a conjunction. (You can write common conjunctions on the board for reference.) To make the activity more challenging, children might like to set a timer. Can they combine their sentences in less than ten seconds? Let children read aloud their combined sentences and tell why they chose the particular conjunction.

Punctuation Bounce

A ball gives students a hands-on lesson in using end punctuation and capital letters.

Gather students in a group and pull out a basketball. Begin bouncing it around the group, and ask children what the ball is doing. (Bounce it hard so it rebounds, at least as high as your head.) When they reply "The ball bounces up high," ask what punctuation mark the ball reminds them of. Establish that "When you put a period (the basketball) at the end of a sentence, it will bounce up high indicating the need for a capital letter to begin the next word." Silly, but it helps students remember this new skill!

Charlotte Sassman
Alice Carlson Applied Learning Center
Fort Worth, Texas

Literature LINK

Bing Bang Boing

by Douglas Florian (Harcourt Brace, 1994)

This delightful collection of poems includes the eight-line "Commas" (see page 137), which gives children a great visual for remembering what this punctuation mark looks like—it's the one with claws! For a related activity, see page 122.

TIP

Tests that include sections on conventions of language often include a passage with punctuation and/or spelling mistakes for children to edit. Children might be asked to highlight errors, then write the appropriate punctuation above them. To help students organize their approach to such a task, teach them the "Beginning and Ending" strategy: Check the beginning of sentences for capitals, then check the end of sentences for end punctuation.

Commas With Claws

After sharing the poem "Commas" with students (see Literature Link, page 121), let them bring their own commas to life.

- Share "Commas," by Douglas Florian, along with the illustrations that accompany the poem. (See page 137.) Ask students why they think the poet likens commas to claws.

- With this visual in mind, let students create commas that are as alive as those in the poem. They might turn them into catlike creatures, even dress them up in the "comma pajamas" mentioned in the poem.

- Let students find commas in books they're reading. Invite them to share ideas about how commas can help make sentences easier to read and understand. For example, writers use commas to separate ideas and items in a series, to separate cities from states and months from dates, and to set speakers apart from quotations.

- Have students find an example of a comma used in one of these ways and write the sentence next to their creative comma picture. Create a display that students can easily refer to when they're wondering about using commas in their own writing.

Quiet Quotations

This quiet activity is surprisingly fun—it teaches the use of quotation marks without anyone speaking at all!

Pair up students after teaching a lesson on using quotations. Have students write back and forth to each other four or five times (for about 10–15 minutes), using questions and answers with quotations and dialogue tags. What makes the activity really fun is requiring that no one speak aloud at all. Students must write everything! (Keep the focus on using quotation marks, and off spelling and other skills for now.)

Charlotte Sassman
Alice Carlson Applied Learning Center
Fort Worth, Texas

Comic Captions

Funny photos can bring out the comedian in us. They're great to use while teaching children about quotation marks.

Look for funny photos in newspapers and magazines. Invite students to find them, too. Cut out the photos and display them a few at a time on a bulletin board. Provide copies of the word bubbles on page 138. Let children use the word bubbles (with quotation marks) to tell what the person in the photo is saying. Have children display their word bubbles next to the corresponding photos for an amusing classroom display.

Macaroni Marks

Elbow macaroni becomes a memorable manipulative in a literature-based activity that teaches the use of quotation marks.

Copy a familiar text (a selection from the Frog and Toad series, by Arnold Lobel, works well) on chart paper. Leave out the punctuation marks. Lead a discussion about where the periods should go. After letting children take turns filling them in, talk about what Frog and Toad are saying. Guide children to notice that it's difficult to follow who is saying what without proper punctuation. Demonstrate the use of quotation marks by gluing two pieces of elbow macaroni at the beginning of the first conversation. Ask children to tell where the end of that thought is. Place two more pieces of macaroni there. Continue, asking children where pieces of the dialogue begin and end and gluing macaroni in place accordingly. Children will remember that "quotation marks are like macaroni" as they continue to place macaroni where each quotation mark would go.

Charlotte Sassman
Alice Carlson Applied Learning Center
Fort Worth, Texas

For dozens of displays that build grammar skills and more, see *Interactive Bulletin Boards: Language Arts*, by Judy Meagher and Joan Novelli (Scholastic, 1998).

Name _____   Date _____

Rhyming People, Places, Things

Read the nouns. Fill in the blank with a rhyming
noun or noun phrase. The first one shows you how!

1. A can, a pan, and a **man named Dan** _____.

2. A stack, a track, and a _____.

3. A bank, a prank, and a _____.

4. A jet, a net, and a pet named _____.

5. A mop, a drop, and a sign that says _____.

6. A string, a ring, and a king who can _____.

7. A sock, a rock, and a clock that goes tick _____.

8. Our town, a crown, and a clown in a _____.

TRY THIS!

Create your own rhyming noun set. Write it here. Leave a blank so a
classmate can fill in a noun.

The Great Big Idea Book: Language Arts © 2009, Scholastic Teaching Resources

Name _____   Date _____

Noun-a-Morphs

Dear Family,
We're studying parts of speech in class—including nouns and proper nouns. Try this activity with your child to learn about nouns that need capital letters. To complete the activity, your child needs to "morph" each noun to make it a proper noun, then highlight each capital letter.

Noun		Proper Noun
author		Dr. Seuss
boy		
girl		
street		
day		
month		
book		
city		
state		
country		

Name _____   Date _____

Alphabet Countdown

A	N
B	O
C	P
D	Q
E	R
F	S
G	T
H	U
I	V
J	W
K	X
L	Y
M	Z

Name _____   Date _____

Pronoun Bingo

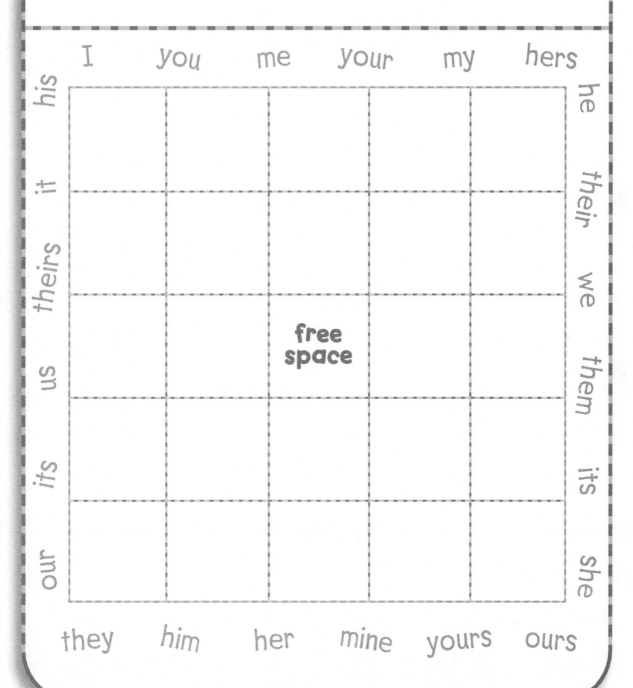

	I	you	me	your	my	hers	
his							he
it							their
theirs			free space				we
us							them
its							its
our							she
	they	him	her	mine	yours	ours	

Name _____ Date _____

Adjective Detectives

What's in my sock?
Read the clues and
then guess!

Clue 1 _____

Clue 2 _____

Clue 3 _____

Lift the flap to
check your answer.

Tape flap here.

The Great Big Idea Book: Language Arts © 2009, Scholastic Teaching Resources

Name _____ Date _____

Adjective Olympics

1st Place in

_____

Awarded to

_____

on

_____

Name _____   Date _____

Adjective

_____

Synonyms

_____

_____

_____

4

I'm in a thesaurus,
Look and see!
Here are some
adjectives
That tell about me!

by _____

1

3

2

Synonyms

_____

_____

_____

Adjective

Synonyms

_____

_____

_____

Adjective

The Great Big Idea Book: Language Arts © 2009, Scholastic Teaching Resources

Name _____ Date _____

Colorful Caterpillars Grow Long

Name _____   Date _____

Adjectives About Me

I am a ⬜ boy.   I am a ⬜ girl.

My eyes are _____ .

My hair is _____ .

I am _____ than a _____ .

I am _____ than a _____ .

I am more _____ than a _____ .

I am good at _____ .

I am better at _____ .

I am best at _____ .

Who am I?

Tape flap here.

The Great Big Idea Book: Language Arts © 2009, Scholastic Teaching Resources

Name _____ Date _____

Dunk, Dive, Slide!

Name _____   Date _____

Clap, Wiggle, Stomp

Dear Family,

Music is a natural with children, and integrating it with skills and concepts in other parts of the curriculum can help reinforce learning in memorable ways. Here's an action-packed song you can sing with your child to practice verbs. Repeat the song to try the new actions (listed below).

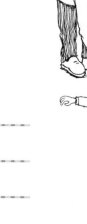

If You're Happy and You Know It

If you're happy and you know it, clap your hands,

If you're happy and you know it, clap your hands,

If you're happy and you know it,
then the whole wide world should know it,

If you're happy and you know it, clap your hands.

Actions for Our New Verses

_____

_____

_____

_____

TRY THIS!

Can your family think of a new action for the song? Write it here. Sing it together!

The Great Big Idea Book: Language Arts © 2009, Scholastic Teaching Resources

Name _____

Date _____

Grammar-Gories

Adverb	Adjective	Future-Tense Verb	Past-Tense Verb	Common Noun	Proper Noun	Letter

Name _____ Date _____

Flipping Over
Parts of Speech

Staple

Staple

The Great Big Idea Book: Language Arts © 2009, Scholastic Teaching Resources

Name _____   Date _____

Commas

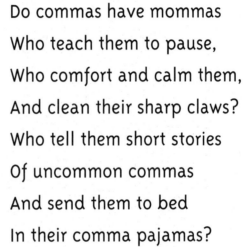

Do commas have mommas
Who teach them to pause,
Who comfort and calm them,
And clean their sharp claws?
Who tell them short stories
Of uncommon commas
And send them to bed
In their comma pajamas?

—Douglas Florian

"COMMAS" from BING BANG BOING by Douglas Florian. Copyright © 1994 by Douglas Florian.
Reprinted by permission of Harcourt Brace.

Name _____ Date _____

Comic Captions

The Great Big Idea Book: Language Arts © 2009, Scholastic Teaching Resources

Spelling

Spelling is one of those skills with which children, teachers, and parents often struggle. Is invented spelling okay? For how long? What's the best way to learn conventional spelling? To assist you in helping students in grades 2–3 achieve the standards for language arts as they relate to mechanical conventions, the activities in this section include spelling high-frequency and commonly misspelled words, spelling phonetically regular words, using a dictionary, and using contractions, suffixes, prefixes, roots, and syllables.

Direct instruction can range from lessons that reinforce phonics skills to those that promote word analysis, teach rules, and integrate application to daily writing. This section is designed to help you provide instruction in those areas through activities that tap into the many ways students learn. For example, Musical Spelling Chairs gets students moving to music as they write collaborative stories with spelling words. (See page 153.) The Art of Spelling combines artistic appreciation and expression with spelling instruction. (See page 166.)

Who Am I?

Your students will happily practice spelling with an irresistible game that lets them get up and move around to learn their words.

- Write each spelling word on a self-stick name label. The words can come from a theme students are studying—for example, oceans. Or you might choose words from other sources, perhaps words that exemplify a rule you are teaching. Make one label for each student.

- Without letting students see the words, place a label on each child's back or forehead.

- Have students mingle, asking one another yes or no questions about their words. The goal is for students to uncover the mystery words on their labels, without being told what the words are. To find out spelling-related clues, students might ask questions about the number of syllables (Do I have more than two syllables?), the beginning sounds (Do I start with a letter that is between A and F?), vowel sounds (Do I have more than one vowel?), and so on.

Post the list of spelling words for reference. Or, to increase the challenge, don't display the words but make sure students have had time to become familiar with them.

What's the Word Worth?

Which spelling word is worth the most points? This activity encourages children to pay attention to each letter in the word to answer this question.

Assign the numbers (values) 1 through 26 to the letters of the alphabet (A = 1, B = 2, C = 3, and so on). Give children each a strip of adding machine tape. Have them record the letters and their values on the paper and tape it to their desks for easy reference. Model the activity by selecting a word, such as a child's name, then assigning points to each letter and adding them up. For example, the name Emma would be worth 5 + 13 + 13 + 1, for a total of 32 points. Give children a list of words to study, then ask them to guess which word will have the greatest value. Let students calculate the sum of the letters for each word, then compare their results. Which word was worth the most? The least?

Sue Lorey
Grove Avenue School
Barrington, Illinois

Skill-Building Beginnings

Try this beginning-of-the-year assessment to help children internalize spelling rules and conventions, rather than memorize a random list of words.

- At the beginning of the school year, administer a baseline evaluation of children's spelling abilities. To do this, select 20 words that reflect specific spelling patterns and rules that students will learn throughout the year—for example, *pickle* (for the ending /kle/), *view* (for the /iew/ vowel sound), *tack* (for the ending /ck/), and *kiss* (for the double *s* at the end of a word). For a sample baseline evaluation, see page 169.

- Say the words one at a time and have children write them down, sounding them out to the best of their abilities.

- Repeat the same word evaluation in the middle of the school year and at the end of the year.

Charlotte Sassman
Alice Carlson Applied Learning Center
Fort Worth, Texas

TIP

Share results of the spelling assessments with families at conference time. They appreciate seeing how the spelling instruction relates to the skills children are mastering, and how their children are progressing.

ENGLISH Language LEARNERS

If you use a weekly spelling list, make modifications to meet the needs of your English language learners. For example, you might select only content words from the list, leaving off function words. If you generally ask students to write a sentence to go with their spelling words, you might ask English language learners to draw a picture of their words instead.

I Spy Spellers

Students have fun making a simple prop that they can use to build spelling skills with the poems, charts, books, and other reading material they use every day.

- Cut card stock into 4- by 6-inch rectangles, then cut out the center of each to make a window. Give one to each child.

- Have students glue or tape the frame onto one end of a craft stick. Students can decorate their I Spy Spellers to add a personal touch and write their names on the craft sticks.

- When you get ready to read the morning message, a poem on chart paper, charts, big books, or other materials with the class, have everyone get their I Spy Spellers before gathering around.

- After sharing the text, take time for some wordplay. Say, "I'm looking for the word [fill in the word of your choice]," and invite one child to come up and use the I Spy Speller to frame the word. Repeat the exercise with new words so that each child has a chance to find a word.

- To vary the activity or focus on spelling patterns, say "I'm looking for a word that [fill in a feature of the target word, such as 'ends in -*ing*']." Again, let children take turns finding and framing the words.

Ann Flagg
Edu-Prize School
Gilbert, Arizona

Three Cheers for Spelling

This lively game helps children associate the shape of letters in words as a memory aid for learning spelling words.

Invite students to suggest body movements to represent "tall" letters (such as *t* and *h*), "hanging" letters (such as *j* and *q*), and "middle" letters (such as *a* and *c*). For example, they might reach to the sky for tall letters, touch their toes for hanging letters, and place hands on hips and jump both feet out (as in a jumping jack) for middle letters. Have a volunteer be the cheerleader and lead the class through a spelling word, shouting out each letter and making the corresponding movement. The word *pet*, for example would have the following movements: toe touch (*p*), hands on hips, feet apart (*e*), reach to the sky (*t*). Spelling out the week's words in this way will give students a welcome chance to be active and will help them associate the letters in a word with their shape.

Hide-and-Seek Spelling

Phonics rules include many spelling patterns for vowel sounds—for example, a vowel followed by a consonant and a silent *e* will have a long vowel sound. This activity introduces students to the multiple ways of spelling a given vowel sound and also helps them recognize words that break that pattern or rule.

⊚ Write a word on chart paper that demonstrates a vowel sound you want to teach—for example, use the word *cake* to teach the silent-*e* rule.

⊚ Ask students which vowel they hear. (*a*) Ask them if it is long or short. (*long*) Share the rule that goes with this sound-spelling pattern and invite children to suggest other words that fit the pattern. Record these on the chart paper.

⊚ If students suggest a word that breaks the rule—for example, *way* or *prey*—write it in a new column.

⊚ Once children see what you're doing with the word lists, turn the action over to them with a game of hide-and-seek: Divide the class into pairs or groups, and let each group "seek" words "hidden" in their books, their own writing, or in print around the room that contain a given sound. Have students record the words they find. Remind them that they must spell the words correctly. If they think of a word that is not in a text, let them consult a dictionary or check their spelling with you.

⊚ Bring students together to share their words. Award a point for each word they find. Record the class total. Set a goal to break that record the next time you play!

Janet Worthington-Samo
St. Clement School
Johnstown, Pennsylvania

You might award bonus points for words that represent a new way to spell the sound.

Lift-the-Flap Weekly Words

Here's an easy-to-use lift-the-flap form for recording, pretesting, and practicing weekly spelling words.

◉ Make a copy of page 170 and record the week's spelling words in the center column. Using this page as a master, photocopy a class set. Prefold students' papers, placing the right column over the center column to conceal the spelling words. Paper-clip the folded section closed.

◉ Give each child a form. Have children write the words in the first column as you read them aloud.

◉ When you're finished with the pretest, let children unfold their papers to reveal the correct spelling of each word. Have them check their papers, matching up words on the left and right and circling any misspelled words. Have students then write misspelled words in the third column.

◉ Encourage children to supplement the spelling words each week with U-Pick Words (see page 147) or words from their spelling folder. Give them a sheet of paper cut to the width of one column on the lift-the-flap spelling form. Have them tape it to the bottom of the third column, then write in their own words.

Wendy Wise-Borg
Rider University
Lawrenceville, New Jersey

TiP

Make it easy for children to practice their spelling words wherever they are by having them write the words on an index card. It's easy to stash the card in a pocket, so children can take it anywhere and study their words whenever they have a few free minutes—for example, in the car on the way to a friend's house or waiting in line at the grocery store.

Tell and Spell

Here's a quick guessing game to play when you have a few spare minutes or just need a change of pace.

Write spelling words on chart paper or the board. As an alternative, you may also write the words on large index cards and make a word wall with them. To play, give students a clue about one of the words—for example, if the word is *believe*, you might say that this word ends in a silent letter. (Choose clues that will reinforce spelling strategies.) Give additional clues until a student guesses the word. Let this child choose a word and give the class clues about it.

Take-Home Activity:
Spelling Skill Builders

An activity page packed with fun ways to practice weekly spelling words encourages students and families to work together at home to strengthen spelling skills.

Make a class set of page 171 and give one to each child. Discuss the activities so that children can explain them to their families. For example, students can play "What's Missing?" by writing each word on a slip of paper and then studying the words before a family member secretly takes two words away. The child then tells which words are missing and spells them. Or students can write their words using a different color for each syllable (great for focusing on word parts). Encourage children to post these activity sheets on their refrigerator at home (or in another handy spot) and use them each week to practice their words.

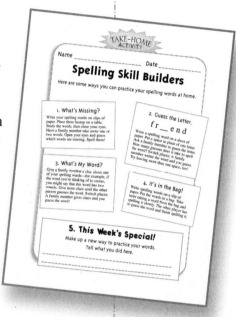

Literature
LINK

Miss Spider's Tea Party
by David Kirk (Scholastic, 1994)

"One lonely spider sipped her tea while gazing at the sky. She watched the insects on the leaf and many flying by." Rhyming words abound in this book about a spider and the guests she invites to tea. Worried that they may end up as Miss Spider's snack, all but one guest decline the invitation. Spiders are carnivorous creatures, but in a surprise move, Miss Spider serves cupcakes with her tea—and gets out the word that she's not to be feared.

A Web of Words

Children are drawn to webs, and a web in their classroom will be no exception. This one will catch students building spelling skills as they explore word families and other spelling patterns.

- After sharing *Miss Spider's Tea Party* (see page 145), ask students to recall some of the rhyming words in the book. Write them on chart paper and invite students to notice any spelling patterns they see. For example, if they suggest *may, day, stay,* and *away,* they'll notice that each word contains the letter cluster *-ay*.

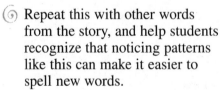
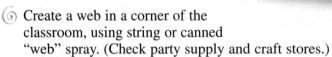

- Repeat this with other words from the story, and help students recognize that noticing patterns like this can make it easier to spell new words.

- Create a web in a corner of the classroom, using string or canned "web" spray. (Check party supply and craft stores.)

- Introduce a new spelling pattern or rule and brainstorm words that have this spelling. Write the words on spider-shaped cards (see page 172) as students say them, and place them in the web.

- Place blank spider-shaped cards at the web so that students can add new words from their reading and writing that fit the spelling pattern or rule.

- Review the words (and any exceptions to the rule or pattern) every few days. When it's time to introduce a new pattern, replace the spiders with new ones.

TIP

Make it easy for students to review spelling patterns and rules at the web by placing on a binder ring words you take down. Students can flip through the words, reading them aloud and quizzing a partner on the spelling.

U-Pick Words

This customized list of spelling words lets each student set spelling goals throughout the year.

- Type up a list of 50 of the most-used words in children's writing for your grade. (For a sample list, see page 173.) Pretest students on the words over a period of a week or so. (Ten words a day might be enough.)

- Check students' papers, then give each child a copy of the list with the words highlighted that he or she misspelled.

- Invite students to choose U-Pick words from their highlighted list to supplement other spelling word lists you assign.

Wendy Wise-Borg
Rider University
Lawrenceville, New Jersey

Alpha-Order Movers

When your students need to know how to spell a word, the dictionary's a great place to go. This activity teaches a skill that will make that trip to the dictionary a lot more likely.

Write spelling words on index cards, one word per card. Give students one card each, and then let them practice arranging themselves in alphabetical order. You can try to accommodate the whole class, giving each child a card, or give cards to half the class at a time to make the task more manageable.

Wendy Weiner
Parkview Elementary School
Milwaukee, Wisconsin

Thematic Picture Dictionaries

When students' spelling words come from topics they're writing and talking about, there's added motivation to learn to spell them. Build a collaborative picture dictionary, complete with spelling tips, to integrate language arts connections throughout a theme unit and increase the number of words students learn how to spell.

- As you explore a theme unit, such as one on insects or deserts, build a list of related spelling words.

- Give each child a sheet of drawing paper. Have children each select a word to illustrate. Ask them to write the word on the paper, use it in a sentence related to the theme, and include any "secrets" they have about how to remember the correct spelling. For example, a child illustrating the word *beetle* for a picture dictionary about insects might suggest that classmates remember the double *e* by telling themselves there's a *bee* in *beetle*.

- Gather children in a seated circle and let them share their dictionary pages and spelling tips. Punch holes in the pages and place in a binder to make a book. Add additional pages as the unit continues. Students who think of new spelling secrets can add them to the back of each page.

TIP

Let students arrange their dictionary pages in alphabetical order. When more than one word starts with the same letter, teach a mini-lesson on alphabetizing. On index cards, write words that start with the same letter and let students practice placing them in order.

ENGLISH Language LEARNERS

Creating personal picture dictionaries can help English language students learn spellings for words that name people, places, and things they know. Place sheets of drawing paper in a binder to make the dictionary. Have children start with words for people, places, and things they know. These might include names for family members, types of pets they have (*dog, cat, fish*), sports they play (*soccer, basketball, baseball*), games they like, as well as objects they use at school (*backpack, pencil, book, ruler*). Write the words in the dictionary and have students trace them, or write them on a separate sheet of paper and have students copy them. Let children illustrate their words to provide visual clues.

Find It Fast

Students are sometimes reluctant to use a dictionary as a spelling resource because they don't know quite where to look. Try this activity to help them develop dictionary skills that will let them find what they're looking for more quickly.

Teach a mini-lesson on using guide words in the dictionary. Help children understand that by knowing how to use guide words, they can more quickly find the page a word is on. Ask children to write each spelling word on an index card and pretend each is a dictionary page. To practice using guide words, have them find two words in the newspaper that could be guide words on each "dictionary page." Remind them that the words must start with the same beginning letter. Like guide words, alphabetically one must come before the spelling word and one must come after. For example, if the spelling word is *stripes*, the guide words could be *snow* and *swing*. Have students cut out their guide words and glue them to the top left and right corners of the corresponding spelling cards.

Sue Lorey
Grove Avenue School
Barrington, Illinois

High-Frequency Word Wall

Try this approach to ensure that your classroom Word Wall does not become a Word Corridor.

When there are too many words on a word wall, it becomes unmanageable and unhelpful to children. To avoid this, try a word wall limited to high-frequency words. These are words children will use often in their writing. They'll learn to check their spelling against the Word Wall, remembering over time right where to find the words they're looking for.

Charlotte Sassman
Alice Carlson Applied Learning Center
Fort Worth, Texas

Share this test-taking tip with children to encourage them to check their spelling. When they're finished writing all their words, have them "Look, Cover, Write, and Check" by looking at each word, saying and spelling it (quietly or to themselves), then covering it with their nonwriting hand and writing it again next to the original. Have them lift their hand to compare the spelling.

Poetry Wordplay

Let poems from *The Pig in the Spigot* (see below) inspire students' own experiments with rhymes, puns, and wordplay. They'll have fun writing, and focus on spelling as they look for their own little words in big words.

Give each child a copy of the poems on page 174. Read the poems aloud together, then look at them closely—for example, can students find any rhyming words? Puns? Other kinds of wordplay? What smaller words can they uncover in bigger words? Let students team up to write their own poems that hide little words in big words. They don't need to worry about using rhyming words, though if they want to use one, a rhyming dictionary can be a big help. (See Tip, left.)

Literature LINK

The Pig in the Spigot

by Richard Wilbur (Harcourt, 2000)

This collection of playful poetry lets readers have fun discovering shorter words in longer words—for example, there's an *ouch* in a mother kangaroo's *pouch*, a *bug* in *bugle*, a big *tree* in the middle of the *street*, and a *sea* in *nausea*. (See page 174 for sample poems.) Because your students won't want to stop playing around with the poetry in the book, it's a great time to engage them in writing their own wordplay poems. (See Poetry Wordplay, above.)

Big Words, Little Words

This favorite activity helps children attend to specific letters in words they're learning and build word analysis skills.

- After sharing *The Pig in the Spigot* (see Literature Link, page 150), turn students loose to search for little words in big words. Make a copy of page 175. Write a spelling word in the squares at the top of the page (one letter per square). Give a copy to each child.

- Have children cut apart the letters in the squares and use them to form new words. Ask them to record their "little words" in the spaces provided.

- Bring students together to share words they found. How many sight words could students make? Other words? For more spelling fun, share *There's an Ant in Anthony*. (See below.)

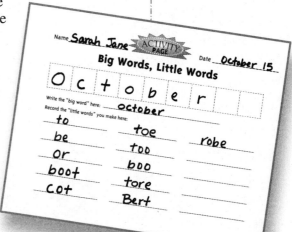

Name **Sarah Jane**   ACTIVITY PAGE   Date **October 15**

Big Words, Little Words

| O | c | t | o | b | e | r | | |

Write the "big word" here: __october__
Record the "little words" you make here:

to	toe	
be	too	robe
or	too	
boot	boo	
cot	tore	
	Bert	

Literature LINK

There's an Ant in Anthony

by Bernard Most (Morrow, 1980)

Anthony is surprised to find an ant in his name, then goes on to find an *ant* in *plant, antenna, hydrant, elephant, phantom, Atlantic,* and more. After sharing the story, challenge students to find words in their classmates' names. For example, they might find an *am* in *Kamiko,* a *jam* in *Jamal,* a *car* in *Carly,* a *pet* in *Peter,* and an *ace* in *Dacey!* Now can they find those same little words in other words? For example, the *pet* in *Peter* is also in *carpet, petunia, puppet,* and the seabird *petrel.*

Snake and Spell

This hands-on spelling activity combines computer-printed words with everyone's favorite—play clay!

Print out sight words in outline form and big type. Laminate each word. Set out the words and a bucket of play clay. (See recipe, left.) Invite children to practice spelling their words by making "snakes" with the clay and molding the snakes to the shape of each letter.

Ann Flagg
Edu-Prize School
Gilbert, Arizona

Play Clay Recipe

This play clay keeps well in resealable plastic bags.

2 cups flour

1 cup salt

2 cups water

4 tablespoons cream of tartar

2 tablespoons vegetable oil

food coloring

Mix ingredients in a pan and stir over medium heat until a dough forms. Let the dough cool slightly, then knead. Add food coloring as desired.

Rainstick Relay Spelling

This fast-paced game challenges children to find words fast—before the sound of a rainstick runs out.

Grab a rainstick (the music teacher might have one if you don't) and gather children around a list of spelling words on chart paper or the board. Say a rule or feature of a spelling word, turn the rainstick upside down to start the sound, and pass it to a child. Have that child take the rainstick and, before the sound is over, find, point to, and spell the word. Say another rule or feature of a spelling word, and have that child pass the rainstick to another student, who repeats the procedure. Start the rainstick over as needed so that everyone has a chance to find, point to, and spell the target word, with plenty of sound left in the rainstick.

Musical Spelling Chairs

This version of musical chairs lets students build a collection of collaborative stories that feature their spelling words.

- Post a list of spelling words. Ask students to copy the list on a sheet of paper in any order they like—the more mixed up, the better.

- Have students write their names on their papers, then use the first word on their list in a sentence to start a story. Ask students to cross that word off the list.

- Start some music and have everyone get up and move around the room. When you stop the music, have children sit in the closest seat and add to the story, making sure to use the next word.

- When they've had enough time, start up the music and have students get up and move about the room again. When you stop the music, have them quickly sit in the closest seat and use the next word on the list to continue the story.

- Repeat until you reach the last word on each child's list. Tell students that when the music stops this time, they need to find a seat and use the last word to finish the story.

- Over the next few days, let children share their stories aloud. Expect some laughs and creative story lines.

TIP

Enhance your spelling program with more games. Click on Language Arts at **www. lessonplanspage .com** and scroll down to the spelling section for teacher-submitted ideas. Check back often for updates!

ENGLISH **Language** LEARNERS

Whenever you plan a gamelike activity to reinforce spelling skills, make sure your English language learners can succeed at it. For example, in the above activity, students are all working within the same time frame to write their sentences, which may be especially difficult for a English language learner. You might let that child dictate the words to you or work with a partner to help tell each part of the story. Have the child read back the words to reinforce word recognition.

Spelling's in the Bag!

Have students partner up for a fun game that lets them practice their spelling words in context.

- Give each set of partners a blank grid. (See page 176.) Have partners work together to write their weekly spelling words on the grid, one letter per box. Students can fill in any leftover boxes with words of their choosing. It's not important that they fill in all of the squares. Have students cut apart their words, keeping each word intact.

- When students have their grids filled in, give them a separate grid you have made ahead of time containing 20 high-frequency words (such as *the*, *because*, and *which*). Have students cut apart the words on this grid, again keeping words intact. Ask children to put all their words in a brown paper lunch bag.

- To play, each player should draw 3 words form the bag. Next, the first player rolls a die and takes that many words out of the bag. The object of the game is to create a sentence using four or more of the words. Players get one point for each word they use in a sentence.

- After each player takes a predetermined number of turns (say, four), the round ends. Players return their words to the bag, shake them up, and play a new round.

Becky Hetz
Waterford Elementary School
Waterford, Pennsylvania

Stack and Spell

This computer-based activity lets children combine words, pictures, and sounds to reinforce spelling words.

Create a HyperStudio (Knowledge Adventure) stack with movable letters. Students drag the letters to make their spelling words, then draw a picture on the HyperStudio card and Save As: [child's name] Spelling Stack. Another option is to have children create their own movable letters to make one spelling word on each card. Then have them add a sentence and draw a picture using that word. Adding sounds will enhance the cards and add another layer to the learning!

Lorraine Leo
Jackson School
Newton, Massachusetts

Fill a Word-Family House

Students fill this house with words that reinforce spelling patterns.

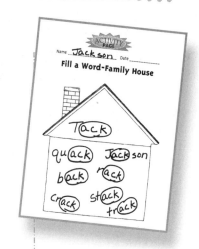

- Give students copies of the template on page 177. Have them choose two words from their spelling list that have the same spelling pattern—for example, *pet* and *net*. Ask students to write these words in the roof section and box the letters that represent the pattern (-*et*).

- Have students add new words that fit that spelling pattern in the remaining part of the house. Ask them to box the letters that make up the pattern in these words, too.

- As students get to more challenging spelling lists, they may have words that could be a part of more than one house—for example, the word *purple* could go in a roof of one house. The student could box the *ur* and come up with words with that pattern, such as *fur* or *furniture*. A student could also box the letters -*le* in *purple* and add words such as *tickle* or *sparkle* to the house.

- If students add words with the proper sound but incorrect spelling—for example, the words in the roof are *wait* and *bait*, and the student records *lait* in the section below, ask him or her to think of another way to spell the same sound. Let the child put the correct spelling on the outside of the house, and explain that even though it has the same sound, it belongs to a different word family.

Wendy Kerner
Edity Teter Elementary
Fairplay, Colorado

Literature LINK

Spots: Counting Creatures From Sky to Sea by Carolyn Lesser (Harcourt Brace, 1999)

What's a counting book doing in a book about spelling? With leopard rays "flapping, looping, cruising," jaguars "slinking, prowling, hunting," seals "sunning, slipping, diving," and wrens "warming, waiting, hatching," this playful picture book is the perfect tool for teaching the suffix -*ing*!

TIP

Students may include words in their house that do not fit the pattern—for example, if the pattern is -*et* as in *pet*, a child might include the word *feet* (because it also has the letters -*et*). Help children recognize that these words belong to different families.

155

Add an -*ing*!

Students become -*ing* experts by working backward—looking at words that end in -*ing* to discover the rule for adding it.

🌀 After sharing the book *Spots: Counting Creatures From Sky to Sea* (see page 155), let students take turns writing the action words from each spread or set of pages on the board. (There are three words that describe movements for each of ten animals featured.)

🌀 Read the words aloud together, and then ask students what the words have in common. (*They end in* -ing.) Explain that this is called a suffix. Invite students to suggest other suffixes they know—for example, -*ed* and -*s*.

🌀 Have students take turns telling what each word on the board would be without the suffix—for example, *looping* is *loop* and *waiting* is *wait*.

🌀 The list also presents you with lots of opportunities to teach irregular endings. Guide students to notice that without the suffix, *sunning* is *sun*, *slipping* is *slip*, and *diving* is *dive*. Invite students to suggest spelling rules for these words. For example, if a word ends in a silent -*e*, drop the *e* before adding a suffix that starts with a vowel (as is the case with -*ing*). Double the last letter of one-syllable words that end in consonants, before adding -*ing*. Challenge students to think of other words that fit those rules. Try them out!

Moving, Saying, Spelling

Take a cue from the book *Spots: Counting Creatures From Sky to Sea*, and let students move to their own -*ing* words.

Invite students to think of a way they can move—for example, hopping, skipping, dancing, creeping, tiptoeing, and stomping. Have them each write a movement word on a slip of paper (check the spelling), then place the papers in a bag. Shake up the bag, and let children take turns selecting a slip of paper and demonstrating the movement without naming it. Let the first classmate to guess the movement write the word for it on the board and take the next turn. Follow up by revisiting the rules students learned in Add an -*ing*! (See above.) To which of their words did they just add -*ing*? To which did they need to add or drop a letter before adding -*ing*?

Students might like to turn their new list of movement words into a collaborative book. Each child can write a word (or more) on a sheet of drawing paper and illustrate it. Put the pages together to make a book.

Spelling Rules Make News

"Rebels Win in Overtime!" "Garden Store Opens" "Peace Talks Continue" Headlines are full of words that can help you teach the "silent -*e*" ending. Try a newspaper scavenger hunt to reinforce this basic spelling rule.

- Divide the class into small groups, and give each a newspaper, a large sheet of paper, scissors, glue, and a highlighter.

- Have students scour the newspaper for headlines that include words that end in -*e*. Have them cut out the headlines, glue them to the paper, and highlight those words.

- Bring students together to share their words. Help them sort in two columns those that end in silent -*e* from the others.

- Encourage students to look for more headlines that contain words with a silent -*e*. Cover a bulletin board with newspaper and let students display their headlines on strips of black construction paper. Read them together.

Take-Home Activity:
Spelling Rules Scavenger Hunt

Send home a scavenger hunt to inform families about the rules your students are learning and to reinforce them at home.

Photocopy a class set of page 178. Give each child a copy of the scavenger hunt and review the rules. Let children read the sample words that fit each rule and explain why they fit, then suggest other words they might find that also fit those rules. The scavenger hunt asks that children find one word that fits each rule, but you can encourage children to find more. They'll have fun cutting out words from newspapers, magazines, food packaging, and so on.

TIP

Use the Spelling Rules Make News bulletin board to reinforce other basic spelling rules. For example, challenge children to find words in headlines that represent plural spellings, including plurals of words that end in -*y* (in which case, students will discover that the *y* changes to *i* before adding -*es*).

64-Square Spelling

Challenge children to connect as many of their spelling words as they can with a crossword puzzle game.

Create 64-Square Spelling game boards using copies of the blank grid on page 176. Have children play in pairs, taking turns writing a spelling word in a row of squares (across or down) on the board. After the first word has been written on the grid, all other words must intersect with at least one other word. Players continue taking turns until one player can no longer connect a word. Children can play so that the winner is the last player to connect a word, or they can play cooperatively, counting up the total number of words they connected. The same pairs of players might like to try the game a second time, attempting to increase the number of words they connect by placing them in different positions.

TIP

Let children share their completed game boards with one another to compare strategies for connecting words.

ENGLISH Language LEARNERS

Like crossword puzzles, word searches can be a fun way to practice spelling words. Creating word searches lets English language learners practice writing their spelling words and then reinforces the spelling as they do their own word search. This would make a good activity for English language learners to share with the class. The template on page 176 works well for word searches, as does large-square graph paper.

Go Dog, House, Boat

Learning to recognize compound words makes spelling more manageable for students. This game lets them play with compound-word construction.

- ☺ Invite students to review the rules for the card game Go Fish. Explain that this game is similar to that.

- ☺ To play, divide the class into several groups of 2–3 children each. Give each group a set of pages 179 and 180. Have children cut apart the cards, shuffle them, and deal seven to each player. Remaining cards are placed facedown in the center.

- ☺ The first player asks another player, "Do you have a [name a compound word part]?" If the child has this card, he or she gives it to the player taking a turn. The player places the compound word faceup on the table. If the child does not have the word, the player selects a card from the center, again placing any compound words faceup on the table.

- ☺ Play passes to the next player, who repeats the procedure. Continue until all cards have been played and children can't form any more compound words.

- ☺ Have players finish up by reading their words aloud. Encourage them to notice words among the players that have the same word part—for example, there may be more than one word with *house* in it.

TIP

For a challenging whole-class version of a compound game, say a compound word. Let a volunteer say a different word that shares the first or second word in your compound. Have another student build a new compound word with one of the words in the previous child's compound word. Continue, letting students take turns coming up with as many linking compound words as they can.

The *qu-* Challenge

The letter *q* always provides a challenge in a game of Scrabble. Because it's worth 10 points, nobody ever wants to give it up—or end up with it at the end of the game. But even with a *u*, it's not always easy to spell those *qu-* words. This game gives students an advantage the next time they play this favorite game by teaching *qu-* spelling patterns.

⑥ Write the *qu-* rule at the top of a chart: *Q* is almost always followed by *u*.

⑥ Have students find and cut out *qu-* words from magazines and newspapers and paste them on the chart. Students can check samples of their writing for more examples.

⑥ Give students practice using the *qu-* rule (and building a good *qu-* vocabulary for Scrabble) by posing a *qu-* Challenge each day. Write letters that can be used to make one or more *qu-* words on the board. (Scramble the letters.) Assign each letter a number of points, and post this information. Based on Scrabble, for example, A, E, I, O, and U are worth 1 each; the letters P, M, and B are worth 3 each; the letter K is worth 5; the letter C, 3; and so on.

⑥ As part of their morning routine, challenge students to use the letters to make *qu-* words. What is the highest value word they can make each day? Take time to let students share the words they make. Record words on chart paper to build a ready spelling reference.

Literature LINK

My First Book of Sign

by Joan Holub (Troll, 1996)

This beginner's guide to finger spelling and sign language features the sign for each letter of the alphabet as well as signs for words that begin with each letter.

Look for more fun ways to reinforce spelling skills at **atozteacher stuff.com**. It's a great site to visit for those times you have a few free minutes. Students will enjoy the quick games and get in some spelling practice at the same time.

Spell It, Sign It

Introduce students to sign language with *My First Book of Sign* (see page 160), and give them a new way to practice their spelling words.

- Give students a copy of the alphabet hand signs. (See page 181.) Model the sign for each letter as children follow along.

- Choose a spelling word to practice. Say and sign each letter in turn. Let children repeat the word, saying and signing each letter.

- Once children are familiar with the idea of signing letters, divide the class into groups and assign each group a word (but don't let anyone know what the other groups' words are). Have children in each group practice signing their words, with each child signing a different letter. (Depending on the number of students in the group and letters in the word, students may sign more than one letter per word.) Remind students to sign the letters in order.

- Let each group sign the word for the class. How quickly can the class "read" each word?

As an extension, and for more practice with the sign language alphabet, invite a volunteer to sign a spelling word for the class each morning. Encourage children to keep the word to themselves once they get it so that everyone has a chance to figure it out.

Outlaw Words

Although many words follow a specific pattern, some break all the rules. Help students recognize "outlaw words" with this activity.

Outlaw words crop up when you are teaching children to identify a spelling pattern. For example, you ask them to name words in the *-at* family, and, inevitably, someone suggests the word *what* because it looks as though it fits the pattern. Explain that outlaw words have the same letters as the pattern but they sound different. Challenge children to search for these rule-breakers in books and other print material that you share. When they discover one, add it to a display of "Outlaw Words." This becomes a handy spelling resource for students.

Colleen Huston
Poca Elementary
Poca, West Virginia
Adapted from Scholastic *Instructor*
(March 1999)

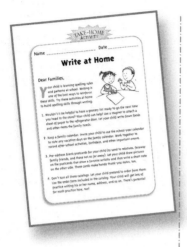

Acrostics are a fun way for children to tackle tough spelling words. For example, to learn the word *height* (which children will discover doesn't fit the "*i* before *e*" rule), children might make up an acrostic that goes like this: Harry's elephant is going home tomorrow.

Take-Home Activity:
Write at Home

Writing improves spelling, and there are many opportunities in everyday life to do just that.

Ask children to name ways their families use writing—for example, to take phone messages, write letters, make a grocery list, complete forms, record important events and appointments on calendars, and write checks. Photocopy page 182 for students to take home. Review the assignment with students, explaining that for a week you want them to try at least one of the writing activities daily. Give children time each day at school to comment on the real-life writing they're doing. Can they remember any words they had trouble spelling? Any words they learned how to spell?

Spot the Syllables

Does every syllable in every word have a vowel or *y*? Challenge children to prove this spelling rule true or false with this activity.

Write spelling words on chart paper. Have children take turns breaking them into syllables by highlighting each syllable in a different color. Give students a few minutes to see if each syllable has a vowel or *y*. If the answer's yes, ask them if they think they can find a word that breaks this rule. After students have had time to try out the rule on as many words as they like, ask them how knowing this rule can help them become better spellers. For example, they can check words they're not sure of, syllable by syllable, to see if each has a vowel or *y*. If not, does another spelling make more sense?

An Anagram Race

What do the words *hear* and *hare* have in common? All of their letters! Let children play with anagrams (words that have the same letters in a different order) to build word analysis and spelling skills.

Sample Anagrams

swing	wings
smile	miles
hear	hare
spots	stops
desert	rested

⑤ Generate a list of anagram pairs. (See right.) Write one word in each pair on a slip of paper.

⑤ Divide the class into groups. Place four or five of the words in a paper bag for each group of students. Give each group a number and write that number on the bag. Line up the bags at the front of the room.

⑤ Have children get in their groups and have paper and pencil ready. On your signal, have one child from each group race to the bag, grab a word out of it, and bring it back to the group. Have students work together to rearrange the letters in the word to spell a new word. Remind them that they need to use all of the letters.

⑤ Have them record the anagrams on their paper, then send another child in the group to get a new word. Have children continue until they've used all the words and found an anagram for each.

⑤ Bring students together to share their anagrams. Then let them return to their groups to come up with one new pair of anagrams. Have a volunteer from each group write one of the words on the board. Let students try to use the letters in each word to spell a new word.

Literature LINK

Word Wizard

by Cathyrn Falwell (Houghton Mifflin, 1998)

Share this fanciful story to introduce the concept of or have more fun with anagrams. In it, a young girl's alphabet cereal letters rearrange themselves to spell new words. Pass around a box of alphabet cereal or noodles, and let students make anagrams as they listen.

Search and Spell

Here's an easy way for students to make word searches for extra spelling practice.

Give students copies of the grid on page 176. Have them write their spelling words horizontally, vertically, or diagonally, one letter per square. They can fill in any blank spaces with miscellaneous letters. Let students exchange papers and locate the hidden spelling words.

Sue Lorey
Grove Avenue School
Barrington, Illinois

Linking-Letter Tiles

Physically arranging letter tiles is especially helpful for visual learners.

Gather old Scrabble games (they don't need to be complete) from students' families, garage sales, and secondhand stores. Place all the letter tiles together, and let students use them to spell out their words. They'll also have fun counting up the number of points in their words. Which spelling word is worth the most points? The fewest?

Susan Perkins
Susan Appleton Meadville Elementary School
Nathalie, Virginia

ENGLISH Language LEARNERS

It's always better when students can learn something by utilizing more than one of the senses. Letter tiles provide English language learners with a tactile experience, letting them practice spelling words by manipulating the actual letters as well as by seeing them. To start out, give English language learners a letter-tile template (see page 176) that you've filled in with their spelling words. They can then place the actual letter tiles on the template, matching the tiles with the letters to build the words.

Spelling Parade

Break up the usual routine of a weekly spelling list and test by planning a variation of a Vocabulary Parade (see page 22).

Using *Miss Alaineus* as inspiration (see below), invite students to plan a simple costume that represents one of their spelling words. Students can team up to create costumes together. For example, in the book, two students create a costume for the word *magnetism*, with one being the magnet and the other a jumble of nails or tacks. Children might choose to incorporate definitions in their costumes. On the day costumes are due, plan a parade through the lunchroom, library, or hallway. (Or arrange to visit other classrooms.) Wrap up the day by having students create scrapbook pages of their words. (Use the pages at the end of *Miss Alaineus* as a model.) Have them record their word and a definition (again, *Miss Alaineus* provides wonderful inspiration for creative definitions), draw a picture of themselves in costume, and write a caption. Punch holes in the pages and place in a binder to make a spelling scrapbook.

Literature LINK

Miss Alaineus: A Vocabulary Disaster

by Debra Frasier (Harcourt, 2000)

Forest is "not a thicket of trees" but a boy who has a cold, which causes the narrator to catch a cold, which causes her to stay home on Vocabulary Day. Her friend gives her the word list over the phone, including—*miscellaneous*, which becomes "Miss Alaineus" and the beginning of this inventive and educational tale. The story concludes with a Vocabulary Parade Scrapbook, which your students can have fun adapting for use with their spelling words. (See above.)

The Art of Spelling

Famous photographs, paintings, and pieces of music inspire students to use spelling words in stories.

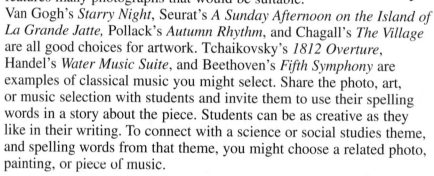

Choose a famous painting, a classic photograph, or a familiar piece of classical music and share it with students. *Life* magazine features many photographs that would be suitable. Van Gogh's *Starry Night*, Seurat's *A Sunday Afternoon on the Island of La Grande Jatte*, Pollack's *Autumn Rhythm*, and Chagall's *The Village* are all good choices for artwork. Tchaikovsky's *1812 Overture*, Handel's *Water Music Suite*, and Beethoven's *Fifth Symphony* are examples of classical music you might select. Share the photo, art, or music selection with students and invite them to use their spelling words in a story about the piece. Students can be as creative as they like in their writing. To connect with a science or social studies theme, and spelling words from that theme, you might choose a related photo, painting, or piece of music.

Randi Lynn Mrvos
Homeschool Teacher
Lexington, Kentucky

TIP

To learn more, share biographies of the artist or composer and explain facts about the painting or music.

Literature LINK

Eye Spy: A Book of Alphabet Puzzles

by Linda Bourke (Chronicle, 1991)

This playful book features a riddle for each letter of the alphabet, while introducing homonyms and homophones. For example, the letter *a* is illustrated with three views of an ant. A fourth picture on the page features someone's *aunt*. Clues to the next letter's puzzle add another layer to the wordplay.

Sounds the Same

Students get two word spellings for one when they learn homonyms—words that sound alike and are often spelled the same.

After sharing *Eye Spy* (see page 166), ask your students to think of other homonyms. Assign pairs of students to create their own illustrated homonym posters modeled on the book (four words to a page). Display the posters as a spelling resource students can consult for their writing.

Wendy Wise-Borg
Rider University
Lawrenceville, New Jersey

Who's on the Homophones?

Your students will teach one another about homophones (words that sound alike but are different in meaning and usually spelling) in this fast and fun game.

- After teaching a mini-lesson on homophones, have students brainstorm as many homophones as they can. (See samples, right.) List the homophones on the board or chart paper.

- Have each student choose a partner and together write a sentence that includes both uses of a homophone. Have them leave blanks where the homophones go—for example, "I was _____ so I asked my friend to play a _____ game."

- Collect the sentences. On paper plates, write each word that will go in a blank (one word per plate). Shuffle the plates and arrange them in a circle on the floor. Have students form a circle around the plates.

- Start some music and have students walk from plate to plate around the circle. When you stop the music, have them stop at the closest plate. Choose a homophone sentence at random and read it aloud. Have students listen to see if the words they're closest to fit in the sentence. If they do, have them hold up those plates. Read the sentence aloud again, this time letting those students chime in the words. Continue, using all of the sentences and words.

Sample Homophones

blew, blue

board, bored

brake, break

by, buy

capital, capitol

cent, scent

dear, deer

dew, do, due

find, fined

for, four

hole, whole

its, it's

knight, night

knows, nose

plain, plane

too, two, to

weight, wait

write, right

Ace Proofreaders, Inc.

What have students learned about the letter combination *ie*? What do they know about adding *-ing* when a word ends in *-y*? Do they know the difference between *there*, *their*, and *they're*? How about *its* and *it's*? As students did in the proofreading activity that focused on grammar (page 119), this time, let them put their spelling skills to the test.

◌ Remind students that even though published material, such as a newspaper, gets proofread, mistakes still happen. Locate a newspaper article that contains a spelling mistake and place a transparency of it on an overhead projector. Challenge children to find the mistake. Provide clues if necessary to lead them to their discovery.

◌ Ask children how many spelling mistakes in newspapers they think they can find in one week. Provide the paper for review each day, and encourage children to look at home, too.

◌ Set aside a bulletin board for students to display their findings. Have them highlight the mistakes and write the correction on an index card, then display both on the bulletin board.

◌ Take time to let students share their proofreading accomplishments. Encourage them to make connections to any spelling rules they've learned. Talk about how they can apply the same skills with their own writing.

Skill-Building Beginnings

The following sample baseline spelling evaluation covers spelling rules and patterns often taught in grades 2–3. Use the blank spaces to add words with other patterns you want to evaluate.

Words		
pickle	running	....
view	jumping	....
tack	making	....
miss	action	....
friend	trees	....
monkeys	tries	....
cake	listened	....
ring	elves	....
wheels	don't	....
lashes	receive	....

Name _____

Date _____

Lift-the-Flap Weekly Words

Pretest	Weekly Words	Words to Learn

Name _____   Date _____

Spelling Skill Builders

Here are some ways you can practice your spelling words at home.

1. What's Missing?

Write your spelling words on slips of paper. Place them faceup on a table. Study the words, then close your eyes. Have a family member take away one or two words. Open your eyes and guess which words are missing. Spell them!

2. Guess the Letter.

f r __ e n d

Write a spelling word on a sheet of paper. Put a space in place of one letter. Ask a family member to guess the letter. How many guesses does it take to spell the word? Switch places: A family member writes the word and you guess. Try leaving more than one space, too!

3. What's My Word?

Give a family member a clue about one of your spelling words—for example, if the word you're thinking of is *cactus*, you might say that this word has two vowels. Give more clues until the other person guesses the word. Switch places: A family member gives clues and you guess the word!

4. It's in the Bag!

Write spelling words on slips of paper. Put the words in a bag. Take turns picking a word from the bag and beginning to spell it aloud slowly. The other player has to guess the word and finish spelling it.

5. This Week's Special!

Make up a new way to practice your words.
Tell what you did here.

_____

_____

The Great Big Idea Book: Language Arts © 2009, Scholastic Teaching Resources

Name _____   Date _____

A Web of Words

Name _____ Date _____

U-Pick Words

1. afraid
2. a lot
3. always
4. another
5. around
6. asked
7. because
8. before
9. believe
10. caught
11. children
12. clothes
13. country
14. decided
15. different
16. eighth
17. everywhere
18. except
19. family
20. favorite
21. finally
22. found
23. friend
24. happened
25. having
26. heard
27. house
28. important
29. instead
30. leave
31. lying
32. might
33. morning
34. people
35. probably
36. said
37. scared
38. school
39. should
40. started
41. suddenly
42. their
43. through
44. thought
45. together
46. trouble
47. upon
48. where
49. whole
50. would

Name _____   Date _____

Poetry Wordplay

The mother kangaroo makes long, long jumps
And comes to earth with very heavy bumps.
That is the reason why, inside her pouch,
Her child is constantly exclaiming "Ouch!"

—*by Richard Wilbur*

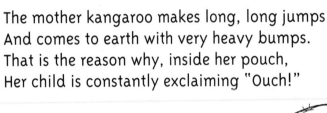

When there's a pig inside your spigot, you
Must not cry out, "There's nothing I can do!"
Be sensible, and take the obvious course,
Which is to turn the spigot on full force.
Sufficient water pressure will, I think,
Oblige the pig to flow into the sink.

—*by Richard Wilbur*

From THE PIG IN THE SPIGOT by Richard Wilbur. Copyright © 2000 by Richard Wilbur.
Reprinted by permission of Harcourt Inc.

Big Words, Little Words

Write the "big word" here: _____

Record the "little words" you make here:

Name _____   Date _____

Name _____   Date _____

Fill a Word-Family House

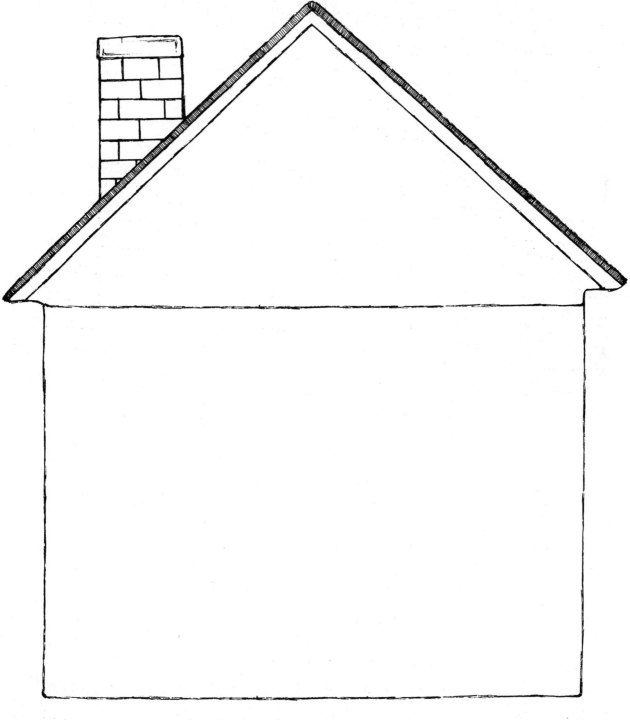

Name _____ Date _____

Spelling Rules Scavenger Hunt

Dear Family,

One way to help your child become a stronger speller is to reinforce spelling rules at home. Try this scavenger hunt to reinforce five useful rules. Work together to find a word that fits each rule; you can look on food packaging, in newspapers, on signs, in books, and so on. (Try to use at least three different sources.) A sample word is given for each.

Please return this paper to school by_____ .

Rule	Sample Word	My Word
1. For most words with an **i** and **e**, it's **i** before **e** except after **c**.	friend	
2. To make the plural of a word that ends in **-y**, change the **y** to **i**, then add **-es**.	sky	
3. To make the plural of a word that ends in **-ey**, just add **-s**.	key	
4. To add **-ing** to words that end in a silent **-e**, drop the **-e**, then add **-ing**.	skate	
5. To add **-ed** or **-ing** to a one-syllable word with a short vowel, you will usually double the final consonant.	run	

The Great Big Idea Book: Language Arts © 2009, Scholastic Teaching Resources

Name _____   Date _____

Go Dog, House, Boat

dog	house	boat
bag	book	mark
sun	light	rise
book	sun	flower
sun	house	shine

The Great Big Idea Book: Language Arts © 2009, Scholastic Teaching Resources

Name _____ Date _____

Go Dog, House, Boat

flash	light	house
light	fire	light
day	house	some
body	day	some
snow	one	ball

Name _____

Sign It, Spell It

ACTIVITY PAGE

A	B	C	D	E	F

G	H	I	J	K	L

M	N	O	P	Q	R

T	U	V	W	X	Y	Z

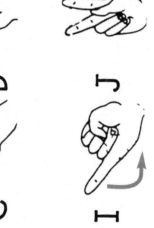

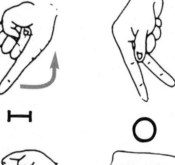
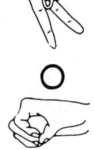

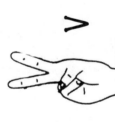
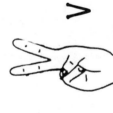

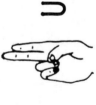

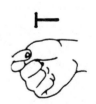

Name _____   Date _____

Write at Home

Dear Family,

Your child is learning spelling rules and patterns at school. Writing is one of the best ways to reinforce these skills. Try these activities at home to build spelling skills through writing.

1. Wouldn't it be helpful to have a grocery list ready to go the next time you head to the store? Your child can help! Use a magnet to attach a sheet of paper to the refrigerator door. Let your child write down foods and other items the family needs.

2. Keep a family calendar. Invite your child to use the school-year calendar to note any vacation days on the family calendar. Work together to record after-school activities, birthdays, and other important events.

3. Pre-address blank postcards for your child (to send to relatives, faraway family friends, and those not so far away). Let your child draw pictures on the postcards that show a favorite activity and then write a short note on the other side. These cards make handy thank-you notes, too.

4. Don't toss all those catalogs. Let your child pretend to order from them. Use the order form included in the catalog. Your child will get lots of practice writing his or her name, address, and so on. There's potential for math practice here, too!

The Great Big Idea Book: Language Arts © 2009, Scholastic Teaching Resources

Listening & Speaking

What do children spend more than half of their school day doing? Reading? Math? Talking? Actually, the answer is listening! According to one study, 57.5 percent of an elementary child's school day is spent listening. Yet the ability to listen is often taken for granted, even though research shows that students who have had structured learning experiences to promote listening have performance scores significantly higher than those who have not.

Tied closely to listening is the form of communication most widely used in school, home, work, and social interaction—speaking. Clear communication through speech, either in presentation or in dialogue with others, is a tremendously important skill that also benefits greatly from experiences designed to help encourage and develop this ability.

More schools and states are now recognizing the importance of listening and speaking as vital components of a well-rounded language arts education. Though writing has long been a part of most state curriculums and assessments, more and more now include listening and speaking components. MCREL summarizes these components, stating that students need to learn to use listening and speaking strategies for different purposes, use a variety of verbal communication skills, and use strategies to enhance listening comprehension.

The activities in this section provide opportunities to teach and assess these skills in fun and creative ways. Many integrate more than one skill from across the disciplines. For example, In the News strengthens listening skills, while also giving students a chance to practice writing skills and keep up on current events. (See page 205.) Weather Report builds speaking skills and strengthens science skills and concepts at the same time. (See page 191.)

Sentence Scramblers

Careful listening is a must when you scramble the words in a spoken sentence and students have to figure out what you said.

- Say a sentence aloud, but mix up the word order. For example, you might say, "I brown like shoes your" instead of "I like your brown shoes."

- Ask students to listen to the scrambled sentence and then write the words in the correct order.

- Invite a volunteer to read the sentence aloud and share a listening strategy—for example, good posture, eyes on speaker, and mentally repeating what you heard. Repeat the activity with a few other scrambled sentences, each time sharing a listening strategy.

- Have students work with partners to make up scrambled sentences of their own. Let them share them with the class for more listening and unscrambling. "Class your fun will have!"

Sounds Like a Poem!

What does a poem sound like? Have your students try this listening activity to find out!

Select a place in your school—for example, the classroom, cafeteria, playground, or library. With clipboards in hand, take your students to this location and have them listen very carefully for a few minutes. Ask them to record any sounds they hear. Let students share the sounds on their lists. Record them on chart paper, leaving off any duplicate sounds. Use the sounds to write a class list poem, listing the sounds line by line and ending with "Sounds like [fill in the place]!" It's great to try this with two very different places that provide a vivid contrast in the sorts of sounds one might hear. Imagine trying this in the library and then in the cafeteria at lunchtime!

Number Listening

Students find out that pennies dropped in a can make a loud sound—but they still have to listen carefully to count them.

- Display an empty coffee can and some pennies. Provide students with pencils and paper.

- Stand behind students (students facing away from you) and direct them not to turn around and to listen carefully. Explain that you are going to be dropping pennies in the can and you want everyone to listen very carefully to determine how many you drop all together. Have students keep tallies to show how many pennies they hear as you drop them.

- Let students physically count the coins to check their answers. Repeat the activity, changing the rate and rhythm of the coin drop. You might also let children trade seats with one another to listen from another spot in the room.

TIP

For greater mathematical challenges, switch to dimes, quarters, or other coins and ask for totals.

That's the Answer. What's the Question?

It's fun to play around with words and sentences. It helps give children a feeling of mastery and control of language. This activity boosts listening and speaking skills, too.

Read aloud a statement—for example, "He was already asleep." Have students discuss the sentence in small groups and create questions that would elicit this target statement as an answer. A suitable question for "He was already asleep" might be "Why didn't he come out to play?" Let groups take turns sharing their questions orally and reading the answer immediately afterward. Ask the rest of the class to listen and give feedback about how well the questions and answers match up.

Because He Loved Her

Students tune in to hear what the hero in this progressive song/poem/chant does next. You can repeat the activity any number of times, with different results each time.

Gather children in a circle. Explain that you are going to say the first part of a statement and that they will chime in on the second part: "because he loved her." Say something like "He ate thirty apples . . ." or "He wrestled armadillos all night long . . . ." Then have children add the ending (". . . because he loved her"). Let the child to your right take a turn, offering a line about the hero and having classmates finish the sentence with ". . . because he loved her." Students can feel free to come up with serious or silly lines—their classmates can say the ending with feeling either way.

TiP

For a surprise listening challenge, after everyone has had a turn, ask students to recall all the things the hero did.

Literature LINK

Book of Riddles

by Bennett Cerf (Random House, 1960)

Share some age-appropriate riddles from this (or another) collection. Discuss with the class what makes a good riddle, then let students try sharing some of their own. Ask students to think of an object, person, or place. Have them write down five clues about their selection. Clues that are progressively more specific work well. Let students take turns reading aloud their riddles and letting classmates guess the answer after each clue. If no one guesses by the last clue, the author reveals the answer.

Blind Directions

This twist on a classic listening activity is always a great way to fill a few spare moments or to provide a skill-building break between longer activities.

Pair up students and have them sit back-to-back in their chairs. Give each child a sheet of paper and pencil. Have one child in each set of partners draw a simple design on the paper, using only six straight lines. This child then describes the design to his or her partner so that the child can replicate it. Students must remain back-to-back during the entire process. Students then compare diagrams to see how close the original and replica are. Which directions worked well? Which didn't? What else would have been helpful to know? Have students switch places and try the activity again.

As students become more proficient at explaining clearly and listening carefully, they can try increasingly complex figures.

Puppet Talk

Some students find it very difficult to speak in front of others, even their own classmates. Puppets are one way to help ease students into public speaking.

Bring in or make a puppet to introduce to students. (It's always fun to have a class puppet in hand—one that occasionally pipes in at the morning meeting, gives directions, shares a story, and so on.) Allow time for students to talk to the puppet. (They almost always readily will.) After the class gets used to your puppet, invite them to bring in puppets or stuffed animals of their own to meet and converse with the class puppet. This playacting provides lots of fun opportunities for speaking and listening in a relaxed atmosphere. Children can then move on to give speeches with their puppets, paving the way for an increased comfort level with speaking independently (without puppet props) in front of others.

Judy Wetzel
Woodburn School
Falls Church, Virginia

Encourage atten-
tive listening with
the Story Circle.
Gather students in
a seated circle.
Begin telling a
story. You might
say something like
"Joanne had
always been curi-
ous about the cave.
However, she had
never been there
before today." Now
"pass" the story to
the student next to
you. This student
continues the story,
then passes it to
the next child.
Students must lis-
ten carefully so
they can add a
piece consistent
with what has come
before. This is a
really fun way to
focus listening,
and stories can
turn out to be very
interesting and
creative.

Telephone

A game of Telephone
is a great opportunity
for teaching the
importance of active
listening.

After sharing the story
The Surprise Party
(see below), provide a
similar experience for students
by playing the game Telephone.
Gather children in a seated circle,
and whisper a message to a student to your left. Have that child
whisper the message to the next child, who will repeat it to the next
student, and so on, around the circle. Take this opportunity to teach
children the strategy of active listening. Through active listening, each
student repeats what the first person said to make sure the message
was understood.

Jacqueline Clarke
Cicero Elementary
Cicero, New York

Literature LINK

The Surprise Party

by Pat Hutchins (Macmillan, 1969)

This book begins, "'I'm having a party tomorrow,' whispered
Rabbit. 'It's a surprise.'" Unfortunately, the animal he whispered
it to thought he said, "Rabbit is hoeing the parsley tomorrow."
As the message is passed on, it gets more and more mixed up.
A natural follow-up to the story, of course, is a game of Telephone.
(See above.)

The Listening Box

A closed box with something rattling around inside is always intriguing. Students will listen ever so carefully as they try to figure out what's inside. This activity works well with a unit about the senses or when used regularly with science lessons to investigate new materials.

- Separately wrap the lid and bottom of a small box. Add a ribbon to the lid for effect.

- Show students a list of six to ten small objects—a marble, a key, a coin, a bead, an eraser, and so on. Have students close their eyes while you place one of those objects inside the box.

- Shake, move, and rattle the box while students listen carefully to identify the object. Give them as many chances to guess as you like, then repeat the activity with a new object.

Literature LINK

Drummer Hoff
by Barbara Emberley (Prentice-Hall, 1967)

This picture book features Caldecott-winning illustrations by Ed Emberley and offers lots of noise, action, and rhyme. Listening for rhyme helps students with reading. It provides a pattern and structure that enhance comprehension. In this story, various members of the army help get the cannon ready for firing. Their names rhyme with the action in each sequence and are fun to read aloud. After reading the story, invite students to help you create a class book that uses their own names in rhyme. You can use first and/or last names—whatever works well with the rhyming and subjects. For example, you might end up with something like this: "Young John Jones ate all the cones" or "Tina Salmastrelli rubbed her belly." Have each student write and illustrate a sentence for the story. Combine these in a book and enjoy reading it aloud together.

TIP

For a really fun homework assignment, have students make their own Listening Box to share with the class. Send home guidelines so that families are aware of the sorts of things students might put inside the box.

Public Speaking Self-Check

It's a good idea to get children to self-assess in any area. Here's a checklist-type rubric you can develop with students to evaluate their own public speaking.

- Ask students to share what they know about public speaking—for example, when they share at morning meeting, what do they need to remember? Students might suggest the following: speaking loudly enough to be heard by all, speaking clearly, speaking slowly, looking at people when they speak, waiting their turn to speak, using expression, and using gestures.

- Record students' ideas on chart paper or the board, then use them to create a self-assessment rubric.

- Encourage students to complete the rubric after giving class presentations. Have them date and keep the evaluations. Compare earlier checklists with later ones to let students see how their speaking skills have grown.

Deborah Versfeld
Village School
Princeton Junction, New Jersey

Literature LINK

Arthur Meets the President

by Marc Brown (Little, Brown, 1991)

Arthur enters a national essay contest and wins! Now he must recite his essay before the president of the United States. At the last moment, the president's helicopter creates a wind that blows the notecards out of Arthur's hands. Can his precocious little sister, D.W., save the day for Arthur? Students engaged in organizing their own talks will relate to Arthur's situation as he brainstorms, writes, and prepares his speech.

A Special Place

Here's an assignment that gets everyone listening (and writing and thinking, too).

Tell students that for homework they will need to write about a special place. Ask them to write at least five sentences that describe this place, but not to name it. Encourage them to use their senses as they describe the place, considering how it smells, feels, looks, and sounds. There may even be things to taste there. Have students write their descriptive sentences on an index card or sheet of paper. When they bring their writing to class, let students take turns sharing their pieces with the class. Can the audience guess the place the writer has described?

Kathryn Lay
Homeschool Teacher
Arlington, Texas

Weather Report

Weather is important to kids. Their main concern is whether they'll be able to play outside; that's a big consideration for a second- or third-grader. Tap into this interest by letting students take turns sharing the weather report.

- Assign each student a day to be the class weather reporter. Write the schedule on the class calendar so that students know when their turn is coming.

- To prepare for their weather report, students will need to listen to a local weather report for the day and take some notes.

- Give students time to practice their presentations before sharing them with the class (or even with the school over the public address system). Encourage students to add their own advice about how to dress for the following day, such as "Tomorrow will be cold and windy, so be sure to wear a warm jacket!"

Karen Bjork (retired)
Portage Public Schools
Portage, Michigan

Something Missing?

In this activity, students need to listen carefully to find out what is missing.

- Have students work in pairs to choose a well-known song, poem, jingle, or rhyme. Explain that they need to write down all the words (or the words to the first few lines of a longer song) and then erase one word. For example, they might choose "The Star Spangled Banner" and write "Oh, say can you see, __ the dawn's early light" (having erased the word *by*).

- Have students present the piece to the class by singing, reciting, or reading it. Remind them to leave out one word. The task of the audience is to listen very carefully and try to identify either from memory or context what the missing word is.

This activity works well when setting up center rotations. After a while, have students submit topics to you for inclusion in the Topic Pick bowl. The topics can become very creative!

Crazy Topic Picks

For some fun and quick thinking anytime, try a Crazy Topic Picks session. Students will enjoy creating these silly presentations, and their classmates will have even more fun listening.

- Fill a fish bowl or other container with small folded pieces of paper. On each paper, write a fun topic such as "My Life on Mars" or "Why Chocolate Should Be Eaten at Every Meal."

- At the beginning of a Topic Pick session, let a few students each choose a topic from the bowl. They should then work for the rest of the period preparing a two- or three-minute speech on the topic, writing simple notes on index cards to organize their ideas.

- Give students time to present their silly speeches. Record them on cassette or videotape for a great collection that students may enjoy sharing at open school night.

Lyn MacBruce
Randolph Elementary School
Randolph, Vermont

Buddy Book and Recording

It's highly motivating and very focusing to write for a specific audience, particularly an appreciative audience. Here's a long-term project that combines writing, speaking, and listening skills, while giving second- or third-graders a chance to share with younger children.

- Explain to students that they will be writing a book of their choice and that the book will be for a younger audience, either kindergarten or first grade. Share some examples of age-appropriate picture books on which children can model their books.

- Over a period of time, have students write and illustrate their books. Help them make a durable cover and bind the pages with bookbinding tape or staples.

- With the help of a parent aide or in a one-on-one meeting, have students record their stories as they read the book aloud.

- As a culminating activity, set up a special day for your class to meet the younger class. Have your students buddy up with the younger children and read their books aloud.

Karen Bjork (retired)
Portage Public Schools
Portage, Michigan

Target Note-Taking

When students watch an informational video or presentation, make sure they get the most out of it and build listening skills with "target note-taking."

Before a lesson or presentation, share your objectives with students. For example, let's say you're studying Antarctica and as part of the lesson, students will be watching a video. Tell students which ideas you want them to focus on specifically, such as: Who were the early explorers of Antarctica? What kinds of animals live in Antarctica? Does Antarctica have a government? Have students jot down these questions on a sheet of paper, to serve as a viewing and listening guide. As they listen, encourage students to take notes that relate to any of the questions. This will help them focus on the important content and retain information you want them to learn.

TIP

At the end of the session, students can present their tapes and books to the kindergarten or first-grade teacher to keep as part of the class library. The younger children will enjoy borrowing and listening to their older buddies' tapes and books.

TIP

When handing out a homework assignment, make an overhead copy of the sheet. Give this special overhead copy to one student, along with an erasable overhead marker pen. This student will complete the homework assignment on the overhead sheet, then use it to lead the "homework checking" the next day.

Listening for Directions

Most standardized tests include a set of directions read aloud by the teacher. These directions are sometimes not written anywhere, and students most likely will hear them only once. Students must listen carefully in order to know what it is they are to do in the testing situation. This is a format unfamiliar to most students and it can catch many off guard. Share this test-taking tip to help prepare students.

To familiarize students with testing procedures in which directions are read aloud, run an occasional practice test following this format:

Tell students that you will be reading the directions only once and that they will not be written anywhere.

Remind them that they will only hear them the one time. Urge them to visualize what they are to do as the directions are read.

Providing students with a few short experiences like this will help familiarize them with this method so they will be ready when they encounter it again in more formal testing situations.

Interactive Morning Message:
Good Morning, Judge

Your students listen to each other all the time, every day, all day long, so they probably know what everybody sounds like. Or do they? To build listening skills, try this engaging activity weekly.

Have students close their eyes and put their heads down on their desks. Now tap three students on the shoulders and have them move quietly to the front of the room. With the other students remaining heads down, eyes closed, point to one of the three students and have him or her say, "Good Morning, Judge." The student can disguise his or her voice if desired. After hearing the student, the rest of the students open their eyes and try to guess which one of the three was the speaker. Make sure to give everyone a turn to be the speaker, then repeat the activity with new students.

Million Dollar Word

The idea of a million of anything is always appealing to students, and with this activity they'll be sure to listen for a word that's worth a million dollars.

At the beginning of the day, select a target word and introduce it to the class. Write the word on the board, then give a definition and discuss the word. Then tell the class that the word is the Million Dollar Word for the day. Ask students to listen carefully throughout the day for the Million Dollar Word. Whenever they hear it, have them give a special signal, such as putting their hand on top of their head or holding up a pretend dollar bill. Try to use the word at least twice during the day. See how many students remember, listen, and key in when the word is spoken.

SOLAR Graphic Organizer

There are several acronyms to help students remember good listening skills. SOLAR is an easy one.

Ask students what they think the letters SOLAR might stand for. Let them guess for a while, then share that they stand for: sit (or stand) up straight (S), open posture (O), lean forward (L), ask questions (A), and repeat what you heard (R). On chart paper, write the acronym and the listening tips for which it stands on chart paper. Invite a volunteer to help you model each listening skill for the class. Stand with this child in front of the class and have a brief conversation. Be sure to clearly demonstrate what each letter stands for. Have students identify the skills each gesture represents. Now model another conversation with the same student, this time doing the opposite of each SOLAR tip. Have students identify the attributes that are missing. As a summary piece, make a copy of page 212 for each student. Have students illustrate each letter of SOLAR on their papers and write in the matching descriptors.

Spot-the-Sound Board Game

Students can practice listening for beginning, ending, and medial consonant and vowel sounds with this simple matching game.

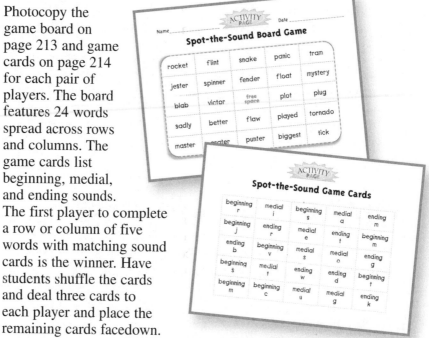

⚙ Photocopy the game board on page 213 and game cards on page 214 for each pair of players. The board features 24 words spread across rows and columns. The game cards list beginning, medial, and ending sounds. The first player to complete a row or column of five words with matching sound cards is the winner. Have students shuffle the cards and deal three cards to each player and place the remaining cards facedown.

⚙ Players take turns trying to match sound cards to words on the board. For example, a player with a "beginning *r*" sound card can place it on the board space labeled "rocket." Have students note that they might be able to place some cards on more than one space. They may also be able to put down more than one card (and they can).

⚙ After completing their turn, players pick up as many cards from the deck as they placed on the game board, so that they always have three cards.

⚙ The first player to complete a row or column of five words, horizontally, vertically, or diagonally, is the winner. It is important for players to realize that the winner is not necessarily the one who puts down the most cards but who completes the row or column. This can involve some strategic thinking as well as sound and letter recognition and matching. Remind students that it may not always be a good idea to place all of their cards down, even if they can.

TIP

Pack copies of the game board and game cards in resealable plastic bags for students to sign out and take home. Review directions with students who take home the game, or type up directions and include them in the bag.

Listening Aesthetically

Music provides the direction in a listening activity that invites an artistic response from students.

- Give students sheets of large white drawing paper and various art materials such as markers, crayons, paints, and colored pencils.

- Choose two musical recordings that are very much in contrast to each other.

- Have students fold their papers in half. Explain to students that you will be playing some music for them and that you would like them to use the art materials to create a picture while they listen. The picture they create will be their illustration of the music.

- Play the first musical selection several times so that students have enough time to hear and translate their impressions to the paper.

- The following day, play the contrasting piece of music while the class uses the second half of their papers to respond to the new music. At the end of the session, ask students to open up their papers and compare and contrast the two illustrations. How are they different? How are they the same? How do their colors, shapes, styles, and subject matter reflect each musical selection?

Literature
LINK

Georgia Music

by Helen V. Griffith (Greenwillow Books, 1986)

This story tells of a girl's visit with her grandfather in rural Georgia. He introduces her to the sounds of Georgia music: bumblebees bumbling, leaves touching each other, grasshoppers and crickets whirring and scratching, and so on. When her grandfather must leave Georgia to live with the girl and her mother, he is lonesome until his granddaughter uses some Georgia music to cheer him up. Ask students to brainstorm a list of sounds that make them feel comfortable, relaxed, or at home. Contrast this with a list of sounds that make students feel uncomfortable, nervous, or scared. Discuss how various sounds can help set a mood or create a character in their writing.

Take-Home Activity:
Word Collectors

It's great to get parents and children involved in developing listening and word-building skills together. This simple activity is designed to get them doing just that.

Give each student a copy of page 215. Review the chart, making sure that children know what kinds of words they're going to collect. You might try a couple in the classroom and model how to fill in the chart before students take the assignment home. When children return their papers to school, let them share the words they found. Record their findings on a master chart. How many different words did they find for the beginning *g* sound? Middle *g* sound? Ending *g* sound? Repeat for the other letters. You might post a class chart for each letter (one chart at a time) and let children continue finding and recording words that fit.

Literature LINK

The Listening Walk
by Paul Showers (HarperCollins, 1991)

In this gently paced picture book, a girl takes a special kind of walk, during which she listens for the great variety of sounds around her. After hearing this story, you might want to take your students on a listening walk. Have them bring along pencils, paper, and a clipboard on which to write. Pause at various points along the way and let students write down some of the sounds they hear. After the walk, compare notes and list all of the sounds students heard.

White Elephant Auction

This activity emphasizes good speaking, writing, and listening in a fun context. It's great for the end of the year.

Explain that a white elephant is something that's silly, unwanted, and generally pretty useless. Invite students to bring in a white elephant object from home. Have them write a description of their object, describing how it could be used or how much fun it would be to have. This is a good activity for encouraging a sense of humor in students' writing voice. Once students have completed the writing, have a "Preview Day," as with a real auction. Arrange the objects, then let students take turns reading their descriptive writing piece to preview each piece. On Auction Day, model the bidding process and provide students with class currency to use. Students will need to listen carefully if they want to get that "special something."

Deborah Bauer
Mesa School District
Mesa, Arizona

Parts-of-Speech Word Stack

This simple but fun activity builds listening and speaking skills as students learn about parts of speech.

- Give each student three index cards. Ask students to write the following labels on the cards (one per card): "Noun," "Verb," and "Adjective."

- On a separate sheet of paper, have students list five words. Four of the words should be the same part of speech and one should be a different part of speech—for example, *cat, dog, boy, desk* (nouns), and *happy* (adjective).

- Let students take turns reading aloud their lists while the rest of the class listens (with their parts-of-speech cards in front of them) for the word that doesn't belong. When they hear the word, have them raise the card with the appropriate part of speech. In this way, everyone participates in every round, either as a presenter or listener. Let a student tell why the word didn't belong, then repeat the activity to let other students share their words.

Randi Lynn Mrvos
Homeschool Teacher
Lexington, Kentucky

As students learn new parts of speech, you can have them add cards to their stack.

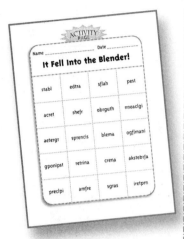

Word List

blast
trade
flash
step

crate
fresh
brought
cleaning

greater
princess
blame
flamingo

stopping
trainer
crane
breakfast

clipper
frame
grass
printer

It Fell Into the Blender!

Learning phonetic concepts has a great deal to do with listening carefully for sounds. Blends are often a focus in second and third grade and are sometimes difficult for students to "hear." This "blender" activity provides some playful practice.

Make a copy of page 216 for each student. Randomly select and read target words from the teacher list (see left) and have students circle the blends on their papers. Wait. That's too easy. Well, the hard part is that these words have fallen into the blender and are all mixed up. Fortunately, the blend is intact but the rest of the letters are scrambled. Students must hear the word and find which mixed-up word fits the word you said aloud, then write it in the space.

Sound Challenge

One of the challenges to listening carefully is background noise that interferes with what we are trying to hear. For example, you might be at an airport listening for a flight announcement but there are also people talking, luggage being wheeled by, and other distractions. Have students practice dealing with this by trying the Sound Challenge.

- Tell students that you are going to read aloud a math problem. This problem will be simple enough to do mentally. They will not need to write anything down, but they must keep their eyes closed while listening. The first time you try this, do it without any interference. Let students share their answers.

- Now have some students be distractors. You might just ask them to have a loud conversation or supply them with musical or rhythm instruments to use.

- While your noisemakers provide the distractions, give the rest of the class another mental math problem to solve. Compare the results and share strategies for focusing even with background noise. You'll have to repeat the activity because everyone will want to take a turn making the distractor noise, providing more listening and math practice for everyone else!

Sequence Listening

Here's a way to practice targeted listening for a series of items.

Give students paper and pencils. Tell them you will be reading a list of items. The items may be numbers, words, or letters. You want them to write down the fourth one they hear. For example, if you say, "Chicago, Detroit, New York, Philadelphia, Los Angeles, Houston, Orlando," students would need to write down "Philadelphia," the fourth item in the list. You can make lists of all kinds of things, such as cities, states, and baseball teams. Alter the ordinal selected as well. After familiarizing students with the activity, let them make lists to read aloud. They really enjoy taking a turn leading the class and will gain some good practice with speaking skills, too!

What's in a Word?

Sometimes just one word can convey a lot of meaning. This connects with some of the more subtle ideas about listening. Not only do we listen to the word or words that are said but also to the way they are said. Have students experience this with a little playacting.

- Ask for a volunteer. Have the student sit down in a chair at a desk. Give this child a play phone to use as a prop. Explain that the student will say one word into the phone, and in that word, will convey a specific meaning. Whisper a word to the volunteer (use the word *no* the first time), and tell that child the mood or feeling you want to convey, such as fear or happiness.

- While the class listens, have the volunteer pick up the phone and say the word in such a way as to convey the intended mood. The volunteer can repeat the word as many times as he or she likes but can say only that word. Let students in the audience guess what the feeling is. How did they know? What kinds of things did they listen for?

- Let students take turns at the phone. Simple words such as *yes*, *no*, *never*, and *sure* are effective, as are short phrases such as *of course*, *not now*, and *very soon*.

Wendy Wise-Borg
Rider University
Lawrenceville, New Jersey

Listening for Literary Elements

Learning about story elements fits very naturally into listening carefully to read-alouds.

There are many great picture book read-alouds for grades 2 and 3. Choose one to read to students, but before you do, introduce and discuss the elements of a story: character, setting (time and place), point of view, mood, and plot. The first time you read the story aloud, just read it as a story to enjoy. Then tell students you will be reading it aloud a second time, and this time you would like them to listen for the various story elements discussed. Ask them to take notes during the second reading. Follow up by discussing the various elements of the story. Encourage children to use their notes as they participate.

A favorite book for this activity is *Do Not Open*, by Brinton Turkle (Dutton, 1993).

Interview Introductions

This is a good activity for the beginning of the year. It helps students get to know each other and builds a cooperative atmosphere as they work together to create a short presentation.

- Give each student a copy of page 217. Assign partners and have students move to quiet areas of the classroom or hall.

- Have partners use the interview guide to gather information and notes about each other. As they ask questions, they should listen to the answers and take notes. (They'll be using their notes to introduce their partners to the class.)

- When all students have finished this phase of the activity, have partners come up to the front of the room and take turns using their notes to introduce each other to the class. This allows students to be introduced to the class without the added pressure of talking about themselves. It gives everyone great practice in speaking, listening, note-taking, and presenting. And by the end of the session, everyone knows a little bit more about their classmates.

ACTIVITY PAGE

Interviewer's Name _____ Date _____

Interview Guide

I am interviewing ....

Age ....

Hobbies, Sports, and Activities ....

Favorite Foods ....

Favorite Books ....

Favorite Movies ....

Dislikes ....

Something Else to Share ....

Art

Kinesthetic Clay Work

Combine creativity, listening, and some math with a project that taps into kinesthetic learning.

2 pyramids
1 sphere
1 rectangular prism
2 cylinders

Give each student a chunk of clay. Tell the class you will be making sculptures together. Each sculpture will be different but will have some of the same elements, mainly certain three-dimensional shapes. Introduce the following shapes one at a time, having students follow your model and make them with their own clay: sphere, cylinder, cone, pyramid, cube, and rectangular prism. Have students describe what makes each shape distinctive, such as the number of sides, number of points, and shape of sides. After students have had a chance to practice making samples of each shape, describe the requirements of the sculpture: It must have two pyramids, one sphere, a rectangular prism, and two cylinders. These can be arranged in any manner students wish. (Record this information on the board.) After students have finished their sculptures, have them check their work to make sure it meets all the requirements. Then let them compare their artwork, noticing how even though everyone used the same shapes, the arrangements have resulted in very different final designs.

Listening Interview

Listening is so intertwined with other skills, it's sometimes difficult to determine if there is a problem with listening or something else. For example, you may ask a student to circle the letter *g* on a paper and she may hear you fine but not be able to visually discriminate the written letter *g* from *d*. To isolate listening skills in an assessment, try an oral listening interview.

Meet one-on-one with a student and ask some simple questions that require only a verbal response. For example, try mentioning some simple words and ask the student to identify the initial, ending, and medial sounds. Is the student able to answer appropriately? How about when you lower your voice? How about if you turn your head and ask the question while looking away? If you suspect there is any sort of hearing problem, an early referral to the nurse for a quick check can be very helpful. Catching a hearing problem early on is key. If hearing is fine but listening is weak, you can provide extra activities in class and as homework to strengthen that skill.

The Music That Inspires Us

This is a good project to connect with a study you are doing about another country or culture.

Bring in a recording that features a particular type or style of music—for example, Brazilian, classical, country, or African. Play some selections for students and let them listen quietly. Then ask them to list things the music makes them think of. List these on the board. Next, tell students you are going to play the music again. This time ask students to think of any colors, images, or moods they "hear." Play the music again, then discuss and list the new ideas. Give students art paper and paints, markers, or crayons. Ask them to create a drawing or painting of some of the images that came to mind from the music. Display the artwork, and invite other classes to visit and view the art while the "music that inspired us" plays in the background.

In the News

Reporters are supposed to give us the five W's (who, what, when, where, why) and an H (how). Do they always? Use a real-life activity to build listening skills and bone up on current events.

⌒ Cut out some newspaper articles. Explain to students that you will be reading aloud an article. You want them to listen for answers to these questions: who, what, when, where, why, and how.

- Give each child a copy of page 218. Have students listen carefully to your reading of the article and write down quick notes that answer very simply and basically the six questions.

- Follow up by having students share what they heard and recorded.

- Now read the news article again so that students can check their accuracy against the story one more time.

- Repeat the activity a few times a week, having students keep their record sheets together. Encourage them to compare their answers to the questions over time. Are they becoming better listeners? How can they tell?

ENGLISH Language LEARNERS

Much of the information we get daily about the news, weather, sports, or events comes to us from listening to the radio or television. Many of the phrases, expressions, and idioms can be very confusing to English language learners. A classic example is "raining cats and dogs." For a homework assignment, ask families of all students to listen to a radio or TV news program together. (Remind families to be aware of the content and to choose something that is appropriate for their children.) Ask them to write down any phrases or words that are idiomatic expressions—that can't be understood by looking at the meaning of the word(s) alone—and to bring them to class. Discuss the idioms or expressions; there are many examples that even native English speakers will have little understanding of. Make copies of page 219. Let students compile the expressions in an illustrated class reference book that all can use.

Interactive Morning Message:
Sound of the Day

Start the day with a morning message that invites careful listening and a little fun.

Before class starts, record a common sound—for example, a doorbell or car horn. Write a morning message that invites students to listen to the sound and write their guess about what it is. After everyone has arrived and had a chance to respond, bring students together as you play the sound again and identify it. Repeat the activity other mornings, using more difficult sounds, such as the hum of a refrigerator or the sound of a pencil moving across a paper. Invite students to create their own sound recordings to be featured as "Sound of the Day."

Take-Home Activity:
Listen Together

This take-home activity pack is designed to foster a school-home connection, while promoting read-alouds, listening, and reading responses.

Label a large resealable plastic bag "Take-Home Activity Pack: Listen Together." Place two age-appropriate picture books as well as a laminated copy of page 220 (a letter to families) and a copy of page 221 (reading response sheet) in the bag. Include a special pencil. (Stickers might be fun, too.) Let children take turns signing it out to share at home. Allow families at least a few days to fit in the activities before asking for the activity pack to be returned. Consider making several copies of the activity pack so that there's less wait time for children to take it home.

Sounds of Poetry

With this activity, students learn that there's more than one way to listen to a poem.

- Give children copies of the poem "Sounds" on page 222. Read the poem aloud, asking students to listen for words that describe how things sound. When you're finished reading the poem, invite children to recall some of those words—for example, *tinkling, buzzing,* and *crunching.*

- Divide the class into small groups. Try to have one group for each sound represented in the poem. Let each group choose a sound from the poem to explore. For example, what would "happy play" sound like? How about "the sound September brings"?

- Give children time to create and practice their sounds. Then bring the class together for another reading. This time, have children make the sound effects at the appropriate times. Compare the two readings. How did students listen the first time? (*by imagining the sounds*) How did they listen the second time? (*by hearing the sounds*)

Easy Listening

Sometimes listening can be difficult. Why? There are lots of things that can interfere. The listener might be tired, the subject might be boring, or the speaker might be going too fast. Use this activity to help students learn what to do when they're having a tough time listening.

Ask students to make two lists: one for things that make listening difficult and one for things that promote good listening. Let students share their lists. Use their ideas to guide a discussion about how students can improve both their speaking and listening abilities. For example, if students understand that talking too fast makes listening difficult, they can set a goal for themselves to slow down when they speak. You might want to generate two charts that summarize students' ideas and use the charts as references for speakers and listeners.

Clap and Repeat

Sound often appears in patterns—for example, the "Beep! Beep! Beep!" of a clock alarm and the barking of a dog. Use the idea of sound patterns in a listening game.

Have students listen carefully to clapping patterns that you present. Begin with simple patterns, such as "clap, clap (pause), clap." Have students repeat the pattern they hear. Make patterns more complex as listening and repeating become more skilled. Add in variations such as finger snapping, knee slapping, or desk tapping. Have students come up with their own variations and lead the class in new patterns. This is a great way to get students' attention. Whenever you begin a pattern of clapping, everyone stops and repeats the pattern. This has students looking, listening, and emptying their hands at the same time so that their focus is complete.

Everyone's Responsibility

It is not uncommon to have a few students who participate in class but in such a way that it is difficult to hear them. Most often, the rest of the class ignores what the hard-to-hear student has said and the teacher ends up asking the student to speak more loudly, slowly, or clearly. Try a different approach to help involve the rest of the class through shared responsibility.

Make it clear that whatever is said in discussion, everyone will be responsible for. For example, if John says the answer is "George Washington," everyone in the class is responsible for hearing John's answer and being able to repeat it. If John speaks too softly, the other students are responsible for asking John in a way that exhibits good manners what it is he said or to please repeat it so all can hear. Model and practice this a few times before making it a standing requirement. You will find that having students work together on this encourages peers to improve their presentation and discussion skills as well as their listening skills.

Evan Milman
Maurice Hawk School
Princeton Junction, New Jersey

Music

Mrs. Martin
Had a Class . . .

Students learn most songs they sing simply by listening.
"Old MacDonald" is one they'll remember.

Write the words to "Old MacDonald" on a chart. (See right.)
Now have fun with the song. Replace some of the words to
make it a little more individualized. So, if your name is Mrs.
Martin, the song might go like this:

Mrs. Martin had a class
A-B-C-D-E.
And in her class
There was [student name]
A-B-C-D-E.
With a [something the student likes to do or is known for] here
And a _____, _____ there.
Here a _____, there a _____,
Everywhere a _____, _____.
Mrs. Martin had a class,
A-B-C-D-E.

Have students write their own verses to share something about themselves. Students will really listen and sing along as this innovative
song comes together.

Literature
LINK

Too Much Noise

by Ann McGovern (Houghton Mifflin, 1967)

A farmer suffers in a house that he believes is too noisy. There are
noises from little things like the wind coming through the cracks
and the tea kettle whistling. The farmer goes to a wise man for
help. The wise man counsels him to bring various animals to
live in the house with him. Things obviously get even noisier.
Children will have fun joining in on all the various sounds that
are repeated throughout the story.

Old MacDonald
had a farm

E-I-E-I-O.

And on his farm

He had a pig

E-I-E-I-O.

With an oink,
oink here

And an oink,
oink there.

Here an oink,

There an oink,

Everywhere an
oink, oink.

Old MacDonald
had a farm

E-I-E-I-O.

Sound Board

Here's a challenging but fun listening activity students will enjoy again and again.

Give each child a copy of the Sound Board, an assortment of 20 different blends and digraphs. (See page 223.) You may want to laminate these to make them reusable, or run additional copies as needed. Tell students you will be saying some words and you would like them to find the box on their Sound Board that has a corresponding sound (specify blend or digraph). Then write the number in that box that corresponds to the order in which the word was said. For example, if the first word you say is *cross*, students will write a 1 in the box with the *cr* blend. Keep a list of the words you say and mark your own copy of the Sound Board as you go. Check the numbers together when you're finished. You can choose the phonetic features you want to focus on and use the corresponding number of words. (Students won't necessarily fill up the board each time you play.)

Alliteration Land

Students enjoy playing with alliterative language. This activity lets them create a town based on the concept of alliteration.

⟳ Share some examples of alliteration from stories. Guide students to recognize that alliteration is a series of words that have the same beginning sound. You might also mention stores, companies, and products that use alliteration to catch people's attention. After all, who wouldn't be interested in Cousin Keith's Crunchy Cookies?

⟳ Tell students they are going to have a chance to try out some alliterative writing on their own. As you give out copies of Alliteration Land (see page 224), explain that students should fill in the sign on each building with an alliterative name. (They can decide what their buildings are—schools, shops, stores, libraries, restaurants, and so on.) Have students draw the product or service offered in the windows.

TIP

Let students arrange their Alliteration Land papers on a bulletin board. Or for a more creative display, let students cut out each building and arrange it, along with roads and other features, to create one giant Alliteration Land.

Stepping Into Stories

Let students step into their favorite stories with Readers Theater productions—a natural for enriching literature studies and promoting speaking and listening skills.

Readers Theater is a great way to help children develop their abilities to read with expression, practice presentation skills, and provide an audience with wonderful listening opportunities. You can purchase prepared Readers Theater scripts, but it is just as easy to adapt appropriate books. The Arthur series, by Marc Brown (Little, Brown), works particularly well. These books feature lots of dialogue and plenty of characters. Provide multiple copies of one of these titles and let children work in groups to prepare presentations.

One or two students in each group can be narrators. These narrators will read any writing that is not in quotation marks. Other students in each group can play the various characters. Have students practice reading the story aloud in their small groups several times before presenting to the class. Remind students that with Readers Theater, there is no need for motions, props, or scenery, just good, clear reading and lots of expression. The audience will be listening to their voices only. In fact, a good culminating activity is to record Readers Theater presentations so they can be seen or heard again and again or used in conjunction with the book for interested readers.

Author Aaron Shepard's Web site (**www.aaron shep.com**) features dozens of ready-to-use Readers Theater scripts. You'll also find detailed how-tos for scripting, staging, and performing Readers Theater productions.

ENGLISH Language LEARNERS

As students learn a new language, they will often be able to obtain meaning early on by focusing on key words. Practice this idea by acting out small scenes. An example might be a scene in a restaurant. Your students want to know the price of a hot dog. What key words will they be listening for in a response? Money words. Number words. If the waiter responds, "Hot dogs are on special today: only 99 cents." Students do not need to understand "special," but if they hear "99 cents," they will have the answer to their question. Have students suggest scenarios in which they might need help. Generate lists of possible key vocabulary that would be important for places such as restaurants, malls, cafeterias, movies, sporting events, libraries, and so on. Review these words and use them as you act out the scenes. When students encounter the real thing, they will be much more well prepared.

Name _____   Date _____

SOLAR Graphic Organizer

Write a sentence that describes what each letter stands for.

S _____

O _____

L _____

A _____

R _____

The Great Big Idea Book: Language Arts © 2009, Scholastic Teaching Resources

Spot-the-Sound Board Game

rocket	flint	snake	panic	tram
jester	spinner	fender	float	mystery
blab	victor	free space	plot	plug
sadly	better	flaw	played	tornado
master	crater	punter	biggest	tick

Spot-the-Sound Game Cards

ending m	medial a	beginning s	medial i	beginning r
beginning m	ending t	medial e	ending r	beginning j
ending g	medial o	medial s	beginning v	ending b
beginning t	ending d	ending w	medial t	beginning s
ending k	medial g	medial u	beginning c	beginning m

The Great Big Idea Book: Language Arts © 2009, Scholastic Teaching Resources

Name _____ Date _____

Word Collectors

Dear Family,

Listening is a very important skill. You can help your child develop this skill in many ways, including with this activity. Work with your child to find a sample word for each of the sounds listed. For instance, the first box asks for a word that starts with the letter *g*. Answers could include words like *guest*, *green*, or *gift*. Say the word aloud to make sure it has the correct sound in the correct place. Complete the page with your child, and have your child say each word aloud.

You'll have a chance to share your word knowledge with your child and your child gets to do the same. Have fun together collecting words!

Sincerely,

_____
Your Child's Teacher

Beginning	Medial	Ending
g _____	g _____	_____ g
a _____	a _____	_____ a
d _____	d _____	_____ d
m _____	m _____	_____ m
e _____	e _____	_____ e
s _____	s _____	_____ s
t _____	t _____	_____ t
r _____	r _____	_____ r
i _____	i _____	_____ i

Name _____   Date _____

It Fell Into the Blender!

stabl	edtra	sflah	pest
acret	shefr	obrguth	nneaclgi
aetergr	sprencis	blema	ogflmani
gponipst	retrina	crena	akstebrfa
preclpi	amfre	sgras	iretprn

Interviewer's Name _____ Date _____

Interview Guide

I am interviewing _____.

Age _____

Hobbies, Sports, and Activities _____

_____

Favorite Foods _____

_____

Favorite Books _____

_____

Favorite Movies _____

_____

Dislikes _____

_____

Something Else to Share _____

_____

Name _____ Date _____

In the News

Who, what, when, where, why, and *how*? These are some of the things you can learn in a news story. Listen to the news story your teacher reads. Jot down information that answers each question.

Title of the Article _____

Reporter _____

Who? _____

What? _____

When? _____

Where? _____

Why? _____

How? _____

TRY THIS!

On your own paper, write a news story about something that happened at school or at home. Does your story answer *who, what, when, where, why,* and *how*?

The Great Big Idea Book: Language Arts © 2009, Scholastic Teaching Resources

Name _____ Date _____

Radio and TV Listening

Word or Phrase _____

What does it mean? _____

_____

_____

_____

Illustration

Use it in a sentence. _____

_____

The Great Big Idea Book: Language Arts © 2009, Scholastic Teaching Resources

Name _____   Date _____

Listen Together

Dear Family,

It is your turn to receive the Listen Together Take-Home Activity Pack. Enclosed you will find two books, a pencil, and a response sheet. You and your child will use the materials to read, write, and listen together. You go first. Choose one of the books to read aloud to your child. Give your child one of the reading response sheets and have him or her write a response to the story. Invite your child to share the response with you. Then discuss the book together. The next night, it is your turn to be the listener. Have your child read the second book to you. This time, you write a response and discuss it with your child. Compare the two books and share favorite parts, characters, illustrations, and so on.

Using these materials will give your child a valuable experience sharing ideas about books with you. It will also enable your child to see the value of reading, writing, and listening. Please return all materials to the bag after completing the activities. Enjoy, and thanks for participating!

Sincerely,

_____
Your Child's Teacher

The Great Big Idea Book: Language Arts © 2009, Scholastic Teaching Resources

Name _____   Date _____

Listen Together

Book 1	Book 2

Book 1

1. Family Reading Partner

_____

2. Book

_____

3. Author

_____

4. Illustrator

_____

5. Response to the Story

_____

_____

_____

_____

Book 2

1. Family Reading Partner

_____

2. Book

_____

3. Author

_____

4. Illustrator

_____

5. Response to the Story

_____

_____

_____

_____

Name _____   Date _____

Sounds

I like the sound of many things—
Of tinkling streams, a bird that sings,
Of falling raindrops, buzzing bees,
Of crunching snow, and wind in trees.

I like the sound of happy play,
Of echoes soft and far away,
Of music gay or sweet and slow,
Of trains and cars that swiftly go.

But there is one sound nicer far
To me than all those others are;
I like the sound September brings
When once again the school bell rings.

—M. Lucille Ford

"SOUNDS" by M. Lucille Ford from Poetry Place
Anthology (Scholastic, 1990).

The Great Big Idea Book: Language Arts © 2009, Scholastic Teaching Resources

Name _____   Date _____

Sound Board

☐ cr	☐ br	☐ cl	☐ bl
☐ gr	☐ gl	☐ dr	☐ fr
☐ fl	☐ pr	☐ pl	☐ st
☐ tr	☐ sm	☐ sp	☐ wh
☐ sh	☐ ch	☐ th	☐ sn

Alliteration Land

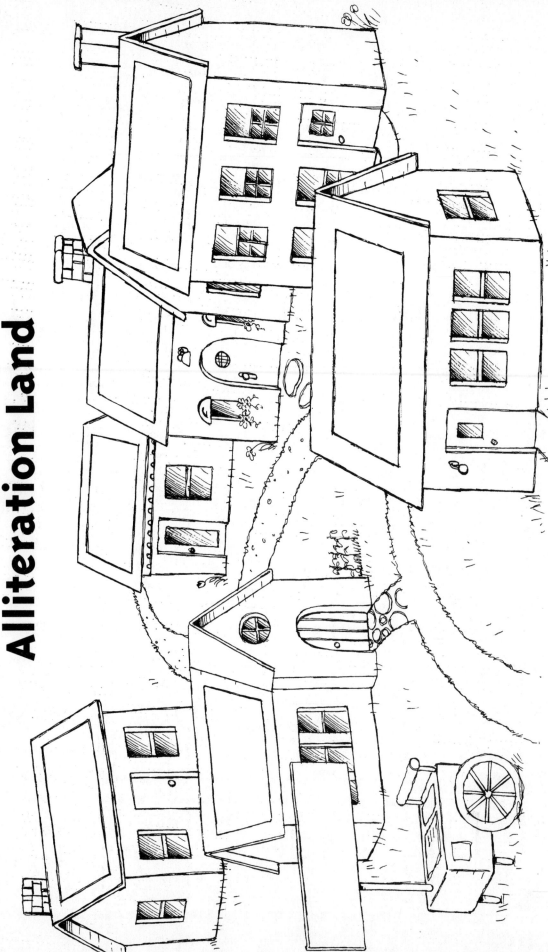

The Great Big Idea Book: Language Arts © 2009, Scholastic Teaching Resources